UNCOMMON FAVOR

Basketball, North Philly, My Mother, and the Lessons I Learned from All Three

DAWN STALEY

BLACK PRIVILEGE
PUBLISHING

ATRIA

New York   Amsterdam/Antwerp   London
Toronto   Sydney/Melbourne   New Delhi

BLACK PRIVILEGE PUBLISHING

ATRIA

An Imprint of Simon & Schuster, LLC
1230 Avenue of the Americas
New York, NY 10020

First Black Privilege Publishing/Atria Books hardcover edition May 2025

BLACK PRIVILEGE PUBLISHING/ATRIA BOOKS and colophon are trademarks of Simon & Schuster, LLC

For information about special discounts for bulk purchases, please contact Simon & Schuster Special Sales at 1-866-506-1949 or business@simonandschuster.com.

The Simon & Schuster Speakers Bureau can bring authors to your live event. For more information or to book an event, contact the Simon & Schuster Speakers Bureau at 1-866-248-3049 or visit our website at www.simonspeakers.com.

Interior design by Davina Mock-Maniscalco

All insert photographs are courtesy of the author except where noted otherwise.

Manufactured in the United States of America

1   3   5   7   9   10   8   6   4   2

Library of Congress Control Number has been applied for.

ISBN 978-1-6680-2336-5
ISBN 978-1-6680-2338-9 (ebook)

To Lawrence, Pete, Tracey, and Eric—
my first friends, first foes, first protectors, and
lifelong supporters. My siblings—who taught me
and continue to show me unconditional love.

To Philadelphia,
for instilling in me the fearlessness to stand,
the toughness to fight, and the resiliency to win.
Without you, I wouldn't be me.

And most of all, to Estelle Staley, my beautiful mother.
It all started with you. Through you I learned to live
courageously, to trust my heart, to walk in unwavering faith,
and to never give up. You were my greatest blessing,
and I pray that I've made you proud.

CONTENTS

Contents

UNCOMMON
FAVOR

PREFACE

I was made for basketball.

I knew from the moment I was old enough to run. Maybe earlier. I can't recall a time when I didn't know it.

When I think back on my childhood, the movie in my head is always basketball. How it drove me every day. Cradling the ball, running the court, passing, shooting, charging, blocking, jumping. Every bit of the game came more naturally to me than breathing.

Basketball allowed me to travel to an imaginary place where everything felt good, everything felt right. My skin fit. My soul sang.

I loved the game with my whole heart.

And so it was that basketball became what I devoted myself to, above all else.

I never cheated on it. I never took it for granted. I didn't care what anybody else was doing.

Not then. Not now.

Come hell or high water, I was going to play.

The Disciplined Person Can Do Anything

The disciplined person can do anything. My mother taught me that.

In truth, she taught me everything that ended up mattering in the long run of my life, even if I didn't recognize those lessons at the time. Estelle Staley was loving, funny, compassionate. She sacrificed her needs to provide us, her children, our wants. She was also the epitome of discipline in every way. A southern, South Carolina–born woman who suffered no self-pity and certainly no fools. Especially in her home.

I was born in Philadelphia, Pennsylvania, on May 4, 1970. My family lived in North Philly, in the Raymond Rosen housing projects. If you know anything about the projects, it's a place where the people who reside there have each other's backs.

From the outside, Raymond Rosen may not have seemed a picture-perfect Mayberry, but to me, my neighborhood felt like a *neighborhood*. Yes, we shared struggles and pain. But we also shared our happiness and hope. Raymond Rosen in the eighties was a world where every adult believed they had jurisdiction to parent any young person. If you were acting out, there were multiple sets of eyes on you. Multiple grown-ups ready to set you straight. All to say, I did not run wild. Quite the opposite.

The Raymond Rosen layout consisted of five apartment towers that loomed over rows of smaller houses that were pressed up tight against each other, like pearls strung on a necklace. We had designated blocks. The first block, second block, third block, and so on up to six. My family lived in a three-bedroom house on the fourth block. It was my mother, Estelle; my father, Clarence; my oldest brother, Lawrence; then Anthony; my sister, Tracey; another brother, Eric; then me, the baby.

The people (us) who lived in the row homes really thought we were something else, because the high-rises were filled with a bit of everything, most of it not good. You'd see feces, urine on the floors. Often the elevators didn't work. A lot of unsavory stuff happened there. I'm not trying to shame the high-rises, but once you crossed the big field that separated the row homes from the towers, anything could happen. You'd hear shots fired. You'd see people running.

On our block, we cared about each other. Everybody had disagreements and misunderstandings, but for the most part, when you moved onto our block, you moved into a community.

There were the Martins, who went to our church. The

Thomases, who were all super tall, with a son they called Big Butter. Mr. Woods, he didn't like noise. He also claimed his own parking space on the street. If someone else pulled into that spot, he would let them have it. There were the Jacksons, the Davises. There was Miss Adams, who cleaned her steps with a toothbrush and cut her grass with a pair of scissors. She'd sit on a tiny stool wearing a housedress and move foot by foot until the yard was uniformly trimmed.

One of my best friends was a guy I called Herb. I was around ten years old when he moved into the projects. He was thirteen, the new kid on the block. I mean, Herb looked like what we would call a noodle. You know, those people who look as if you could get over on them.

Herb dressed nice, premium jeans, polo shirt tucked in with a belt, lotion on his face to the point of being shiny. I tried to tell him, dude, nobody's got time to do all of that. Let's get on out here and play. But Herb wanted to stay clean. I have to say, with love, that he was corny, real, real corny. He just didn't fit into the projects.

Herb and I lived on the same block. We played basketball together. He would tell you that he taught me everything I know about the game, when really, he was just a rebounder. At first, he seemed scared of the people in the neighborhood. When he initially arrived, people would try him. As they would any newcomer who didn't know the rules of the block. It was almost an initiation process. Kids are kids. They're going to take advantage.

I decided to become his protector. Even as a ten-year-old I had an innate sense of right and wrong and an impulse to protect the vulnerable. I took him around to make sure that none of the guys would pick on him. I vouched for him until he found his footing. (To this day, Herb and I are friends. He's a supervisor at a mental health center working with young kids in Philly. He comes down to South Carolina to see our games.)

Every block had a captain, and ours was Miss Jones. Miss Jones looked like a cartoon character. Short, heavyset, in a salt-and-pepper wig that flipped up in the back. She had thick glasses and false teeth she put in on fancy occasions. She had a peach tree in her yard. And yes, we did now and again help ourselves to some peaches when she wasn't looking.

Miss Jones lived in the corner house, prime real estate. She'd been in the Raymond Rosen projects for decades. Her kids grew up there. Her grandkids, too. With this longevity came a fierce pride.

Miss Jones ran the fourth block like a drill sergeant. She didn't even allow her grandchildren to get out of line. Back then, the fourth block could have competed and won against any suburban neighborhood when it came to manicured yards, blooming gardens, and tidy upkeep. If you didn't mow your lawn every week, you stuck out. And if you needed your lawn mowed, somebody in the neighborhood would take care of it. Miss Jones made sure everything was immaculate.

My mother shared Miss Jones's love for flowers. We had flowers all over the house, and mom would plant new ones for every season—annuals, perennials, all bright colors. Her favorite flowers were lilies.

Between my mom and the watchful eye of Miss Jones, the

fourth block stayed fresh, cheerful. That was the overwhelming feeling I had back then about my home. It may have been rough around the edges, but we took care of each other, we looked out for each other. We planted flowers. We cultivated joy.

Most days of my childhood, our neighborhood sounded like school recess. Tons of kids running around, yelling and playing. In the summers we would figure out which house was doing the cooking, and by that I mean preparing lunch for the whole block. When it was my mom's turn, we would go to Murry's Steaks for the meat, and we'd buy cheeseburger surprise. Hamburgers with cheese in the middle. You bit into it, and the melted cheese would ooze out. For a kid, that was a sort of magic trick.

Every Sunday my mother and her friend Miss Marie would buy us kids five single cones of chocolate ice cream (and a double dip of butter pecan for Mom) from a place called Jonesy. When they melted on the walk home, we would lick the paper wrapper.

In the projects you have free heat, free electricity. We were fortunate that we had a few air-conditioning units in our house, too, but you couldn't run them all at once, or you'd trip the breaker. In the summertime, we ran the air conditioner downstairs and made pallets on the floors to sleep.

When it wasn't sweltering hot, my sister and I shared a bedroom. My three brothers shared another. My parents took the third. There was a single bathroom for the seven of us. No shower. We all had to take baths, or you had to wash up in the sink. My father, who worked construction, used to come home and bathe, and then he wouldn't clean out the tub. There were rings upon rings of dirt on the inside. Either you had to scrub all that out, or you did what you could to clean yourself using the sink tap and a washcloth. When it came to chores, everybody dreaded cleaning the bathroom.

Another onerous task was washing dishes. Each kid was assigned a week to clean them. My mother cooked virtually every night, and there were no paper plates. She hated paper plates. Seven people eating at home every night—the dishes piled up. If for some reason you didn't wash the family dishes when it was your turn and Mom arrived home from work to a teetering stack of plates and cups in the sink—watch out and run for cover. The scene was about to get dramatic.

My mother cleaned houses to make ends meet. She did it with pride, like a boss, like the CEO of a Fortune 500 company. I came from a strong woman who believed in doing things the right way, no matter what it was. She saw discipline as the route to self-respect.

We could always hear her making her way up the street, chatting with the neighbors and saying good evening to the people she passed by. Inside the house, we'd scramble. "Mommy's coming up, Mommy's coming up!" We kids could clean that house in three minutes flat, pristine. But there was a time or two when the dishes stayed dirty. When my mom walked in exhausted and spotted that stack of plates, she would march over to the kitchen, take a deep breath, then pick them up one by one and slam them onto the floor.

I mean, Every. Single. Dish. Then she'd go upstairs and leave us to deal with the mess. As you might imagine, there wasn't any cooking going on those nights. We had to fend for ourselves for dinner.

When people ask me to describe my mother, I say she was a giver. That was her essential nature. Her reflex as a parent, as a person, too. My mother cared about everybody. She was social, involved in the community. In the projects they used to call her Miss Stelle, shortened from Estelle. A tremendous cook, she would stay up all night, preparing meals for twenty people, then invite dozens more neighbors over. She could not allow a mouth to go unfed. She was generous that way.

At the same time, she abided zero nonsense from us kids. We had to go to school. We had to do our homework. We had to be in the house by her curfew. There have been times when I've wished I'd been less of a shy kid. But I suspect I would've gotten myself into way more hot water if I had been. My introversion combined with the fear I had of disrespecting my mother, of embarrassing her in any way, kept me from making unwise choices. Probably for the best.

If you did not comply with my mom's rules of order, you felt her wrath, meaning you felt her shoe, you felt an extension cord, you felt a switch, which is an old country weapon, where you take a branch from a tree and slide the leaves off till you're left with a thin reed that, if it snapped your flesh, would sting pretty good. My mother ran a tight ship. If you were good with that, she was good with you.

My mom didn't have to speak very often about what her expectations were, because we already knew the rules. What you never wanted, ever, was to put her in a spot where she felt the need to repeat herself. Now, when she did speak, she would say "Didn't I tell you . . ." as some random object would come across your head.

The biggest no-no in our house was breaking curfew. This could have been for our safety, but that's not how it was presented to us. The rule was posed like, "I'm telling you to be in this house by ten o'clock, period." If you weren't, Mom was waiting for you at the door, at the bottom of the steps. Now, what was she waiting for you with? That all depended on what was close by.

I was a disciplined kid. Like I said, my mother would not have had it any other way. I did what I was supposed to do. I wasn't a rule breaker. (I'm still not.) If you gave me instructions, I followed them. And the only time I didn't was when the hours got away from me while I was playing basketball, and I'd find myself late getting home. After a while, my mom knew to come get me on the court. I was never anywhere else.

My mother didn't love that I missed curfew, but it was the only rule I ever broke. And while I may have been punished for staying out late, it made my mom aware of my devotion to the game.

My father, Clarence Staley, was a different animal. He couldn't wrap his head around my playing. A girl trying to become a basketball star didn't compute for him. He was a southern man at heart; the women he knew cooked and cleaned and raised children and looked after the men. I remember him forbidding me to travel on a basketball trip out of state when I was around twelve. He didn't see the point. Some forty-odd years later and I'm still pissed my dad didn't allow me to go.

In many other ways, we were similar. Like me, my father was quiet, reserved. He didn't let many people into his inner life. He was intelligent and well versed in a lot of areas, but he wouldn't brag about it. He was especially good with his hands and skilled at carpentry, working as a mechanic and a construction worker. One summer, he made us a picnic table for the backyard. If you wanted a fence built in the neighborhood, my dad was your guy.

My mother called my dad Leonard. We kids called him "Cut Money," 'cause he cut the money short. Like, we ate fish Friday nights. My dad was too cheap to get the fish cleaned at the market. He would bring the whole fish home, dump it on the counter, and wait for my mother to prep the meal. That job would ultimately fall to my brother Pete, since he'd worked as a fishmonger and knew his way around a deboning knife.

As generous as my mom was, my father was stingy. When it was his week to give out our lunch money, he would "forget." Thankfully, my mother had hiding places around the house where she stashed cash for us to take to school. She had a way of covering all the bases.

On his off-hours, my dad ran numbers as a bookie. There's a lottery in the inner city. People rang him to put in their numbers, and if they hit, he'd pay them out.

When the money was flowing, my dad would meet up with my granddaddy, and the two would come home drunk together. They'd collapse onto the living room sofa and call out to me and Tracey to come take their shoes off so they wouldn't have to stand up. My granddaddy would yell out, "Donna! Donna!"

Donna? Who's Donna?

I decided I didn't need to answer to that name. Those shoes could stay on.

My father enjoyed his liquor. My dad, outside the booze, was a cool dude. But when he drank, he got demanding, bossy.

Those nights, I avoided him. I wasn't frightened. I just felt uncomfortable around the energy. It's why I don't drink. Even as an adult, I only partake occasionally, and never to excess. I like to stay in control.

My parents knew of each other as teens, when they lived back in Woodford, South Carolina, where they were both born. Families all know each other down there. Everyone has heard of so-and-so who is related to such-and-such. My folks knew of each other, but they hadn't really intersected much.

Once my mom moved to Philadelphia, Dad was quick to follow. They may not have dated in South Carolina, but once they were both in Philly, romance bloomed. They married in 1962. The same year, my oldest brother, Lawrence, was born. I don't think my grandmother liked the fact that my mom was pregnant and unwed, so the nuptials were very much of the shotgun variety.

Lawrence was the bully in the house. The first son, he thought he was next in line under my dad and took that to mean he had the authority to hand down his chores to us. Mom would tell him to clean the kitchen, so he would bark to me, "You got to clean the kitchen."

I'd say, "Mommy told you to do it." Then we would fight. Knockdown drag-outs.

He'd put his hands on me in a way that big brothers do younger siblings; we call it mugging. He'd take his palm to my forehead and mush my head when I didn't do what he told me. I was the one he picked on the most because I was the youngest, and we shared the same birthday, eight years apart. (I couldn't get nothing of my own, y'all!)

My second-eldest brother, Anthony, was the sweetest in the family. He was the most like my mother, wanting to make sure that everybody was okay all the time, their needs met. We called him Petey. "Sweet Pete" is how they knew him in the neighborhood. He passed away in 2021 from a stroke at fifty-seven years old.

My youngest brother, Eric, was the best athlete. Way better than I was. I'm sure when we were kids he saw me as the annoying little sister, not that he ever said it out loud. We were close in age and both sports-obsessed, so no doubt it irritated him that I was hanging around with all his pals. His nickname was Top.

Top could run fast; he could play basketball, softball, baseball. He looked out for me, too. Acted as sort of a protector in the projects. To this day, we're compatible because he's low maintenance. He appreciates the simple things in life. Watching a movie. A glass of wine. Smoking a cigar. We can sit side by side and not talk for hours. An ideal scenario for an introvert like me. Top still plays local-league baseball and softball at fifty-eight.

My sister, Tracey, was born six years before me. The room we shared was tiny. Neither one of us was thrilled with the arrangement. Tracey was a neat freak. She hung her T-shirts on hangers. I kept my clothes shoved under the furniture. Tracey made her bed every morning. I slept on top of the covers so I wouldn't have to make my bed at all.

The pair of us slept in a full-sized bed at first. Then we got bunk beds. I had the top bunk. Eventually, as we got older, we brought the bed down and put the two of them side by side, with a small side table and a dresser. Dad made us a head-board, doors for the closet. Our window opened to a view of a pair of huge pine trees. In the winter we would watch the snow blanket the branches.

Even as a kid, Tracey was a hard worker. She was nineteen when she bought herself a television. Brand-new out of the box. It was brown, and she'd purchased a matching brown stand to set it on. She earned the money from her job at a pet shop. When she wasn't home, my brothers would steal the TV and take it to their room.

As the youngest child, I didn't have much that was origi-nally mine. Everything I had were hand-me-downs from my siblings. It didn't bother me, except when it came to socks. New, clean socks were my prized possessions. When you live with boys, they don't care. They'll wear anything. They'll pull on a sock so crusty it doesn't bend. When they used to come for my clean socks I would flip out. That was always a fight waiting to happen.

Five kids in a house makes everything a competition. To eat was a competition. To get in the bathroom first was a com-petition. I may have been born competitive, but my environ-ment definitely added fuel to that fire. Inside, there wasn't much room to do anything. Which led to a lot of squabbling.

There was zero privacy. I remember we had a ten-foot tele-phone cord we stretched to its breaking point so we could chat with no one eavesdropping.

For the most part, I kept in my shell. I didn't talk because there wasn't a lot of invitation to talk. (Even as an adult, for me there is no such thing as an uncomfortable silence.) No one wanted the opinion of the youngest. My siblings would announce, "You're too young to get to have an opinion. You're just going to do what we tell you to do." It wasn't mean. More that I didn't rank. In the mix of my family, I was largely invisible.

Which was fine by me. I was intensely withdrawn. Especially if I didn't know you. I wouldn't say two words if you were outside my circle. I mean, I probably wouldn't even make eye contact. You wouldn't know you existed if it was determined by my giving you attention.

I was also a bit of a crybaby growing up. All kinds of things made me teary. You could hurt my feelings, and I would cry. You could call me a tomboy, insult me, and I would cry. I cried a lot in front of my family. I also sucked my thumb. My mother ironed her sheets, all the linens in the house. I'd take the edge of the freshly pressed sheet (it had such a silky feel), suck my thumb, and rub the fabric between my fingertips. It comforted me. All to say, I was the most softhearted child. The true baby of the family. But the more I played basketball, the more I discovered that all that anxiety quieted when I was on the court.

The primary way I communicated was through my game. Basketball was me talking. My actions when playing. Basketball was me showing you what I was about. On the court, I was free. I wasn't in the confines of a crammed row home. There was room for me to breathe, run, jump. To release the person I longed to be.

When you are an introvert, you feel more than you can convey. Basketball allowed me to express myself without uttering a word.

When I started playing, I typically tapped in to two emotions: happiness and anger. Both fueled my competitive drive. Competition was fierce in our neighborhood. I was the lone girl in the mix. The guys only accepted me once I proved I was strong-willed enough to throw down. Now, their girlfriends had other ideas. They thought I was there to go after their men. I would roll my eyes, say, "No, I don't want your boyfriend. He stinks. No, really, when we play, he smells."

What interested your average preteen girl could not have interested me less. The boys were having all the fun as far as I could tell. There was nothing in me that was traditionally girly. Every fiber of my soul screamed sports, sports, sports. Before long, my family nicknamed me "Dirt" because it became clear I'd rather play ball than bathe.

I longed to be good before I knew whether I had talent. My dreams were about being the best at what I loved, becoming a college champion, an Olympian. The folks who knew me then ascribe my basketball success to determination rather than innate gifts. They say I was less a born athlete and more of an obsessive devotee.

I can't argue with that. I didn't stumble on a natural aptitude and decide to capitalize on its potential. I was singularly preoccupied with basketball. Driven to the point of fixation, I molded myself into an athlete. I was disciplined with a capital *D*.

In our projects we had what was called the Big Field, which was separated by a six-foot fence from the Little Field. When you're under-resourced you get creative. In the Big Field we sketched out makeshift football end zones with spray paint. We would paint lines and run the hundred-yard dash.

Between the fourth and fifth block there was a light pole where we nailed milk crates with the bottoms kicked out. We would play horse. I mastered bank shots on those crates. I'd stay outside and shoot hour upon hour until I could no longer see the basket through the dark.

I didn't even go home to eat. I'd pop in the corner store, inhale some cheese fries. Or hit up the Chinese joint. You could buy three chicken wings with rice and gravy for two dollars.

Sometimes, if we found two poles and two crates, we would make a full court. We had some mean games on those courts. We used to dunk on them! There were proper cement courts on the Big Field, but the younger generation couldn't play there. You had to earn your spot. Some people never did.

When you grow up in inner-city projects, you often don't see anything beyond what's in front of you. It's like being deep in a valley where the horizon is invisible. Your perspective is limited, and the world shrinks into something very small.

It's easy then, almost natural, to assume you're never going to reach beyond the walls you see every day. You don't even have a vision of what "beyond" could look like. (Especially when I lived there, and the internet wasn't even a thing.) The projects pull you in and keep you there.

We were lucky in that every summer our family would leave Raymond Rosen for a two-week road trip. It was during my dad's vacation. We had a big station wagon. The seven of us would pile in, and we'd drive all the way down to see our grandparents in South Carolina, landing twelve hours later in Woodford. We called it "the country."

When it was time to travel south, we'd load up the vehicle

with supplies. My mom would fry chicken. We'd have sand-wiches. A cooler. It was one of those situations where you didn't want anybody to sit by you in that car, but there was no way to avoid it, we were all squished together, somebody was forever leaning on you, falling asleep, that kind of thing. I rode way in the back. I could lie down. Make myself a fort.

Our destination was my grandparents' house, where my mother was raised. We'd spend time with our grandmother and grandfather, our aunts and uncles, all the many cousins. My mom had sixteen siblings. Compared to the big city, the South was slower, calmer. We felt untethered, like we could run wild.

In Woodford, my grandparents lived on several acres. The cousins kept pigs and chickens. I didn't go out at night. I wasn't trying to run into the animals in the dark. Some of my rela-tives had a trailer, a double-wide, nearby on the property. I was fascinated because it was basically a house on cinder blocks. As a kid, I remember wondering whether that meant you could pick up and go anytime you wanted. Even though it had no wheels.

My mom seemed really content in Woodford. She relished that family time. The ease that comes from being among your people. Everyone says I favored her, but my grandmother scared me. I would describe her as harsh, but my sister, Tracey, says that's ungenerous. She'd paint her as firm. How else was she to run a tight ship with sixteen children in the house? Of course, Tracey was the sole grandchild my grandma allowed to sleep in her bed with her. The rest of us had to find a place on the floor. Little wonder she thought Grandma was nice.

I remember my grandmother would rise early, maybe four

thirty in the morning. They lived on a street that was not paved, so she'd walk to the road to get her ride to town. One of her children would go with her since it was still dark out.

I enjoyed South Carolina in the short term. But I couldn't imagine living there full-time. (Ironic, I know.) After a while, I would be itching to return to the city. Back to Raymond Rosen. Back to basketball.

My cousins would tease us. They thought we were rich because we had a house in the city. We were the equivalent of them in Philly, but in their eyes, what we had sounded fancy. There weren't any pigs. So, I guess they had a point.

Honestly, in some ways we were rich (spiritually, emotionally), though I wouldn't have thought to label it that way back then.

What I did know, even as a kid, was that I wanted to do right by my neighborhood. I wanted to make the people I knew proud. I wanted to impress the guys at the playground. I wanted to show respect to our neighbors. I came of age feeling in my bones the desire to represent my community. To stand proud within it, and to show the world who North Philly was.

Until I could manifest my imagined future of playing basketball as a career, I inhabited my small world to the fullest. I sized up the resources around me and made the most of every opportunity, even if that opportunity was shooting free throws against an empty crate till the sun dipped.

It's a rare gift to find your place in the world as a child. To stumble so early onto the thing that makes you whole. I still remember the antsy feeling I got waiting for my school day to hurry up and end so I could get back to business.

Basketball seemed like a life raft and a magic carpet. A sanctuary and a rocket ship. Young as I was, I knew that basketball brought out the best of me and always would, even before I knew what the best of me could be.

All I wanted was to earn my place on the court.

That, as my mother so often reminded me, would take discipline. And thus, disciplined I would be.

Hope Is a Ladder

I was in eighth grade when I received what I believed was a letter of interest from Dartmouth College. A single sheet, folded in thirds, outlining an opportunity to come play basketball. When I opened that envelope and saw my name on there, you couldn't tell me anything.

Now that I'm in coaching, I know that mailer was simply an invitation to a basketball camp, one of hundreds they send to students all over the country. However, when I was thirteen years old, that brochure felt like a letter of intent.

Against all odds it had found its way into my parents' mailbox in the projects in North Philly. To me, that was an unmistakable sign. (Even as a kid, I was a great follower of signs.) Somebody somewhere had their eye on me as an athlete. It kicked my ambition into high gear. It offered me a ladder of hope. My job was to start climbing.

When I was young, I had two goals. First, I wanted to graduate from college. I didn't know how I would get there or where I'd land, but I wanted that for my family. My mom and dad didn't have college aspirations for us kids because we couldn't afford it. Nobody was really thinking about advanced degrees in our neighborhood.

Second, because I only ever saw women play basketball on television at national championship games and during the Olympics, I wanted those accolades, too. To make my way into the big basketball arenas and, once there, to win.

For any of that to happen though, I first needed to conquer the court at our local recreation center. Located at Twenty-Fifth and Diamond, the center was around the corner from where I grew up and across the street from my elementary school. A modest brick building that hosted after-school and summer programs and legendarily competitive basketball games.

Back then it was called the Moylan Recreation Center. After the North Philly basketball legend Hank Gathers passed away, it was renamed the Hank Gathers Recreation Center.

I viewed Hank as the epitome of hard work. When you watched him play, you saw a person who was going to grind it out more than any other baller on the court. Six foot seven, he was a star at Dobbins Technical High School and earned a basketball scholarship to USC and then transferred to Loyola Marymount. When he was a junior, he became the second player in NCAA Division I history to lead in rebounding and scoring in the same season. His achievement saw him named WCC Player of the Year.

Hank was way prouder of rebounding than racking points. "Anybody can score thirty points a night if that's what he's concentrating on," he would say. "But rebounding is special because it comes from the heart." He also used to call himself the strongest man alive. He'd say it with a smile at the end.

Heading into his senior year, Hank was firing on all cylinders, projected to be a lottery pick for the NBA. His future was bright as diamonds. Then early in the season, on December 9, 1989, he collapsed during a home game against UC Santa Barbara.

Doctors diagnosed him with exercise-induced ventricular tachycardia, a heart abnormality. He was prescribed beta-blockers, which slowed his heartbeat, but also his speed of play. Hank couldn't execute the way he wanted. He was forced to rest and sit out games.

LMU coach Paul Westhead had designed a fast, frenetic approach for his team. He favored full-court presses and ran his players up and down the court, emphasizing speed and sprints. Desperate to get back into peak form, Hank asked his doctors to reduce his medication dosage again and again. He fought through and seemingly recovered, returning to the court.

A month after his diagnosis, in a February matchup against LSU, Hank managed forty-eight points and thirteen rebounds even as he was being guarded by the future NBA icons Shaquille O'Neal and Stanley Roberts. A couple of weeks after, Hank lowered his meds even further, then skipped his follow-up cardiology appointment. The team was heading into the semifinals of the WCC tournament. Hank was unwilling to not give his all to the game.

On Sunday, March 4, with fourteen minutes remaining in the first half, Hank dunked off an alley-oop from the Lions point guard Terrell Lowery. Seconds later, he collapsed at the midcourt line.

"I don't want to lie down!" Hank shouted, trying to right himself.

Then he stopped breathing. He was all of twenty-three years old.

They aired the footage of Hank hitting the floor on ESPN's *SportsCenter*. His mother, Lucille, was in the stands. She was holding a sign with his name on it.

The tragedy of Hank's death was immense, but when I think about him, it's as the embodiment of who we are in Philadelphia. He wanted to make it to the league for his family, and that was cut short. But a lot of us will never forget him.

It was his mother who first said to me, "Hope is a ladder." A tool to lift yourself to a brighter future, but also a tool to lift others by your example. Hank also grew up in Raymond Rosen. His folks believed basketball kept him out of the trouble they saw many of his peers in the projects sliding into. Hank made his way while clearing the path for those around him. He showed all of us what could be achieved if you committed yourself to your dream.

Back when I was a kid finding my way on the court, Hank took notice of me. Sometimes he'd encourage the boys to allow me to play. That unexpected support changed the direction of my life. How I saw myself and how others saw me. Because of that, Hank's legacy lives on in my career. Just as it does in the rec center where we played together. That building remains a place where everybody from the neighborhood still comes together. For me, it's the spot where I know that I'm home.

Beginning around age eleven, I'd walk to the rec center courts to practice, but I could only shoot when the older boys like Hank weren't playing. Any chance I got I'd steal time. When they ran to the far end of the court, I'd shoot a couple of shots. Then they'd race back, and I'd grab my ball and dart off to the side. More than anything I wanted to be the one dribbling the length of the court in the heat of the game, not the weird little kid hoarding moments between runs.

I was an odd child. I didn't even talk. Don't get me wrong, I *could* talk, I just didn't like to. I preferred to communicate through basketball. No surprise then that I practically lived on the court. Any spare moment, I could be found there sharpening my game. I was never lonely with a basketball in my hand.

Like any burgeoning athlete, I was shaping my body as a tool, testing the limits of how strong I was. My game said everything about me that I couldn't. A visual illustration of who I was and what I thought was important. It revealed my determination, strength, fight, my never-say-die willfulness, and most of all, the confidence I couldn't seem to find anywhere else. I became consumed with becoming the best player I could be.

I practiced like it was my job. Shot after shot. Hour after hour.

Over time, I developed a sense of pride. When other kids saw what I could do with the ball, the playground taunts about playing like a girl faded into respect. I knew if I could tough it out through a basketball game in the projects—if I could *excel*—I could survive anything coming down the pike.

In the beginning, I'd hang around with my basketball at the rec center or our neighborhood courts, waiting for the guys to invite me to join a game. When they'd ask whether they could borrow my ball, I'd shake my head. "Only if I play, too."

By 1982, I'd gotten good enough to join a local league, where I competed from age twelve to fourteen. My coach's name was Muhammad. Muhammad was a Philadelphia police officer who ran the Powell Center of the Police Athletic League. Talk about disciplined. On and off the court, he was calm, cool, and collected, always clean-shaven and smelling nice. He gave the impression of a man who had his act together and expected the same from us.

Muhammad wanted to create a great experience for us kids and had a caring heart for all young people, but I think he held a special place for me because I was the only girl in the mix. He acted as a protector when I was up against the boys. A moderating influence on guys' comments and attitudes when there's only one girl playing, and that girl is kicking their ass.

As I improved, some of the boys in the neighborhood started to come to our house looking to play with me instead of my brothers. They'd knock on our door and ask my siblings when I'd be home.

I knew I'd earned their ultimate respect when I no longer had to bring my own ball to the court or stand idle for hours to get chosen for a pickup game in the neighborhood. There had been so many times when I had to practice on the side or hold tight to get some shots up until they went down one end of the court.

Then came the day, the glorious day, when the guys invited me to play in the first ten. Now, that was a badge of honor. When you're able to be a part of the first ten, you don't have to wait around, you don't have to shout, "I got next!" You're already out there, balling out.

I was around fourteen years old when that happened, and man, did it feel like I had arrived. It was something I'd wished for the longest time—to play on the big-boy court and be part of the first ten. I knew from that day on, I was *in*. I was going to be picked. It didn't matter whether twenty-five guys showed up to play, I was going to be in the first game. It shifted my mentality and made me even hungrier to compete. I wanted to guarantee they were never sorry they asked me.

I was naive about sex discrimination back then. I didn't really register gender. All I saw was this righteous sport of basketball that I knew I had to be a part of. I was so detached from the limits of opportunity for girls versus boys that when I was very young, I imagined I could play in the NBA. If I was talented enough, why not? There was no women's league in those years. If the NBA was the only professional gig, then that was what I would strive for. I was already playing alongside the boys, after all.

Soon enough I realized it wasn't a realistic hope, but the fact is, having that hope at all drove me forward. Even a false hope can serve a purpose. Imagining myself in a pro uniform, playing in the premier league in the land provided me what I needed to continue pushing myself to greater heights.

I recall one game back in 1985, when I was an eighth grader at FitzSimons Junior High. I scored twenty-five points with ten assists and ten steals. We were competing in a summer league tournament inside Temple's McGonigle Hall. The then men's basketball coach, John Chaney, came to the gym, and I caught his eye. He was so impressed with my game that he called his assistant coach down to the court to watch. Chaney told his AC he wanted him to see what he was looking for in a point guard when he went out to recruit.

After that, I was invited to join Chaney's weeklong co-ed basketball camps. I was thrilled to be there. I wasn't intimidated by the new company I found myself in. I kept playing as I always had, pushing our team to be better, go harder. Chaney later told the media that was when he knew I was destined not just to play, but also to lead. Who could have predicted then that I would coach alongside him when I took over the Temple Owls from 2000 to 2008? That we'd share tips and strategies? That we'd become peers?

Decades later, when South Carolina won our first national championship in 2017, Coach Chaney sent me flowers. The card read, "You done good!"

After he passed away in 2021, USC had a game against UConn. I decided to wear an oversized black sweater, white dress shirt, and black necktie to honor him. I don't know how many people knew why I was dressed that way that day. But those who did think about Coach Chaney were reminded of his legacy of kindness and the uncommon faith he had in his players. He believed his team could win when no one else thought they could. His hope was a ladder for everyone lucky enough to intersect with him, including me. He taught me so much, but nothing as valuable as the power of belief.

When I think back on the random life intersections like the one that brought Coach Chaney and me together, they feel in some ways preordained. The luck or grace that Coach Chaney happened to stop and watch me, and the opportunities that sprang from that moment, were a kind of uncommon favor. I may have been young, but I could already feel the pull of destiny. I didn't let a single opportunity pass me by. I channeled everything I had into my yearning to win.

To that end, I was extremely coachable. I wanted to be the best. Which meant learning more about basketball. I listened to every word from every coach. Tried every instruction and method and drill and routine. I was a basketball sponge, soaking up knowledge like water. Was I a gracious loser? Hell no. I was a sore loser. I'm a sore loser to this day, but I can handle it better because I can identify why we lost. In my younger years I could not identify the whys, and it made me feel crazy.

I was especially tough on the girls I began playing with when I joined my school teams. When I transitioned from competing with boys to playing on all-female squads, let's just say I wasn't an ideal teammate. You could even say I had an attitude problem. I thought I knew better. In my mind, the young women on those teams were starting at a lower standard than where I'd been. They were soft. My passes were harder and my patience was, well, nonexistent when they couldn't catch the ball. I'd roll my eyes when they'd shake their hands and wince because the pass stung their palms. My read was that these players didn't take basketball as seriously as I did.

I'd been forged on the courts of the projects, going up against all dudes, tall, buff, aggressive dudes I had to prove myself to and be exponentially better than just to get an invite to the party. Having succeeded in that Herculean task made me bigheaded and stubborn. Very, very stubborn. I'm a Taurus, so it came naturally. I viewed my obstinance as an asset. Without it, I would never have survived my trial by fire. Being tenacious gave me a tough skin and kept me in the game. But when it came to being on the girls' teams, I needed to find my way to being a more collaborative teammate.

Around this time there was a Philly radio broadcaster named Sonny Hill, the so-called Mayor of Basketball who was organizing local competitions. He's now an executive adviser for the Philadelphia 76ers. Sonny invited me to play in his celebrated regional tournament. I was in my early teens, and the girls I came up against there were tough as nails, future legends such as Yolanda Laney (who eventually became an all-American at Rutgers), Linda "Hawkeye" Page, (soon to be an ACC champ), and Marilyn Stephens-Franklyn, a leading scorer at Temple. I realized I wasn't the only star in the making. There were other young women out there gunning as hard as I was.

This gave me hope of a different kind. One of a future community filled with peers who shared my dream of basketball greatness. It also lit a fire under my ass.

I can't recall precisely when I realized how talented I was, but during those early games at the rec center and in the local leagues, I noticed folks paying attention to my way of playing. Maybe initially because I was the only girl out there. Then, after some time, I'd hear the applause when I took the court. The oohs and aahs when I executed a no-look pass or a pull-up jumper.

I tried not to focus too much on the cheers. But when somebody's enthralled with your play, when you hear them scream or you sense the wave of their excitement after you score, that's when you really know you're right where you're meant to be.

Outside of my school teams, I kept playing with my neighborhood guys. I stayed short and small, while they seemed to grow bigger, stronger, taller. Good, I thought. It was the most efficient way to train me up. Regardless of their size, I drove right into the paint. I wasn't worried about whom I'd find there, or who would try to stop me. It was the same intractable will that I used to convince myself I could jump as high as they could. I may have been tiny, but I had big hands and an even bigger attitude.

Moving the ball is where I really shined. In fact, passing helped keep me on the court because most guys want to shoot. A lot. They want to score. I figured out real quick all I had to do was show the boys I could—and would—pass them the ball so they could score points, and they'd keep me around.

It's funny to think now about how that psychology set me up to be not only a dominant point guard, but also a person predisposed to give the glory to others. My entire philosophy of boosting success by enabling those around you to thrive was born on my local court, as a route to gain playing time.

In junior high school I joined a travel team. My mom forced Tracey to drive me to and from all the games. She was nineteen. I was fifteen. Tracey resented having to do that, but our mother didn't give her a choice. I was grateful. Traveling allowed me to get a taste of how other venues looked and felt, what the crowds were like. I grew more well-rounded as a player as I drank in the experience. By the time I entered Murrell Dobbins Career and Technical Education High School, I was one of the best players in the country, averaging thirty-four points per game.

The girls' team played in a separate gym from the boys. Our facility offered no courtside seating. Just a balcony that could hold around a hundred spectators. We regularly packed a much larger crowd. Our games were standing room only. It meant the world to me to be seen in my element. The fruits of my labor on full display. Being able to do something at a high level is empowering. Knowing you've cultivated expertise is galvanizing.

By my senior year, we were the best team in the area. We'd won consecutive city league championships, and it seemed as if the whole town turned out to watch us play. I was thriving as a point guard. The seeds of self-possession I'd planted on the Hank Gathers and neighborhood courts had blossomed into a mature confidence that I knew exactly what was needed to lead a team to victory. I watched as my teammates came to rely on my self-assurance. Then began adopting it as their own. Like hope, confidence is contagious. We lost zero games during my entire high school career.

When all was said and done, the little girl who had to elbow her way onto her neighborhood basketball court was named the national high school player of the year.

During my rise to national prominence, I was flooded with hundreds of letters from colleges, as well as solicitations from recruiters. In a few short years, I had climbed that ladder of hope and was waiting at the top rung for my next step.

My home visits began in 1987. Without consulting my mother, I'd made the choice not to host potential coaches in our house. I felt uneasy exposing strangers to my neighborhood, my family, the intimate details of our life in the projects.

My mom quickly figured out no recruiters were coming around. She asked why. I said I was meeting them elsewhere. She pressed me, "Why is that?"

It was a rhetorical question.

I shrugged. My mother exhaled, peered into my eyes, and said, "Dawn, never be ashamed to show where you come from, who you are, or what you believe in, because somewhere out there, there's a little girl you'll inspire to achieve something she doesn't think she can do."

Those words changed me forever. On that day, my mother in her infinite wisdom gave me permission to begin embracing the stage that comes with having a spotlight. Though I was still a young person, she intuited where my career might take me. She advised me to lean into the truth of my life and see all of it as an advantage.

I had no cause for shame. I didn't need to pretend I was anyone other than myself.

From that moment on, I took seriously the responsibility that comes with having a national platform and understanding what a voice like mine could offer. I realized I could represent a ladder of hope for someone else.

Needless to say, I ended up proudly hosting some of the coaches in my neighborhood, at my home and with my family.

Today that same high school gym I played in at Dobbins is named after me. After South Carolina won our first national championship, I returned to my neighborhood and visited the Gathers Recreation Center. I presented them with a replica of our NCAA national championship trophy. The exact size and dimensions. It's proudly displayed in a Lucite case in the welcome area.

I wanted every young person who walked through those doors to know that any dream they dared to have was theirs for the taking. I wanted them to see something real and tangible that spelled out where hard work and discipline can lead. That championship hardware would not exist if not for that gym and the training I did on those rims. If I could do it, so could they.

It's vital that people believe they can come up. Where you begin doesn't have to be where you end. This is not to say there is anything wrong with anybody's given circumstance. More to offer a window into other possibilities. To plant the kernel that if you see yourself in another life or career or environment, you can make that vision real. We all have potential to make multiple ambitions a reality.

I remember when I received my first Olympic gold medal. It was at the 1996 Atlanta Games. Team USA had us dress in a designated ceremony outfit. A white nylon jacket appliquéd with blue and red flames and stars, blue track pants. My hair was pulled back in braids, like Cleo from the *Set It Off* movie. We cradled bouquets of orange lilies and sunflowers as we waited in a row for the awards to be doled out. Teresa Edwards was the first to receive her hardware. I was second.

As they were going down the line I was practically vibrating with excitement. By the time they draped the medal around my neck, I couldn't contain myself. I was repeating "Give me mine! Give me mine!" to the Olympic medal staff, who were very proper. It was so North Philly of me. I patted my chest with my two hands: "Give me mine, give me mine."

Later, I gave that medal to my mom.

Mothers are there for you on the good, bad, and ugly days. If you're lucky, your mother is the person in your world who believes in you the most. Mothers are also the people who humble you. They pay for the sneakers. They make the meals. They dry the tears. They kick you in the pants. They shine a light so you don't trip. They catch you when you do.

When I handed the gold medal to my mother, she initially waved it away. Said she didn't want it. She thought I should keep it, display it somewhere. Almost comically, we passed it between us like a hot potato. Eventually I prevailed, and the gold went home to live in Philly. Which, honestly, is where it belonged.

Weeks after the glory and awe of winning in Atlanta, post reaching the highest international peak one could as a player, I was shocked to find myself slipping into a depression. I'd achieved a goal I'd fantasized about since I was old enough to hold a basketball. I expected to be floating on clouds. But I went home and felt . . . nothing.

I didn't know my own body. My head felt detached. I was exhausted and numb. Sad, but I couldn't cry. It was as if I was watching myself from afar, going through the motions of life.

I was an athlete. Any other time, I could count on my physical self to pull me through emotional rough spots. If I was down, or worried, I'd play basketball, and my troubles would ebb away. Running the court was better than any drug, any therapy. That's why it landed on me like a stadium's worth of bricks when I couldn't shake myself out of the blues. The old tried-and-true wasn't working. I didn't recognize who I was.

Some of the battle was existential. Lifelong aspiration: check. Now what? There was no one I could talk to about my malaise. Everyone assumed I'd be dancing in the streets. That I didn't want to move, never mind celebrate, filled me with a unique embarrassment. I'd won an Olympic gold, for eff's sake. What was wrong with me?

I kept all this to myself. I didn't share that I couldn't function. That I didn't want to pick up a basketball or play. I was due to begin working out with the Richmond Rage for the highly anticipated launch of the American Basketball League (ABL), but I had been drained of my competitive drive. I'm from the projects in North Philly. We can handle whatever it is. In my head I kept repeating a quote Coach Tara VanDerveer used all the time. She may have gotten it from Indiana University coach Bobby Knight. "Mental is to the physical as four is to one."

Meaning, you need to be four times stronger mentally than physically to handle strife in your life. I sat there thinking, *It is so true.* Once your mental is shot, you ain't got a shot.

Eventually, I rang Lisa Boyer, my ABL coach at the time, to say I couldn't come to training camp. It was one of the hardest conversations I've ever had. My face flushed hot as I told her I wasn't capable, that something was wrong with me. I'd never had to do that before.

Boyer didn't hesitate. "Take all the time you need," she said. No judgment, no disappointment, no guilt. She said when I was ready, she and the team would be there.

I took two weeks off. I felt bad because my other teammates were at training camp, and I wasn't. I believed I was letting people down, worried they felt I was getting preferential treatment. Soon enough, the anxiety of disappointing my team spurred me to pack my bags, and I traveled to Richmond.

If hope is a ladder, Coach Lisa Boyer is the one who lowered it for me to climb out of those dark, post-Olympic days. She intuited exactly what I needed to hear to begin breaking free of my melancholy. She released the pressure valve. She showed me grace. Sometimes all it takes is one person to be in your corner to make the difference. Since then, I've done my best to pay it forward.

In 1996 I started an after-school program in the same projects where I grew up. I wanted to inspire academic and athletic success for middle-school girls. Help them become the women they longed to be. The program provided hundreds of girls a path to find their passion, to feel powerful in a world full of chaos.

Then, when I moved to South Carolina, I founded a second program in 2013 called INNERSOLE, which provides new sneakers to children who are homeless or in need. This may not sound like much. But to kids without the resources to buy shoes that fit, it can mean everything.

Since starting INNERSOLE, I've received countless notes

from children telling me, "I can run faster and jump higher," or bashfully confessing, "This is my first pair of new shoes."

In my opinion, there is no better feeling than a new pair of sneakers. To a child who has never had their own, unused pair, those shoes represent a path to pride. I know from experience a confident kid can do anything.

The point here is service needn't be a grand show or a huge statement. Service can be a look, a smile, a gesture of empathy, a show of respect, a hug, a two-week break, a new pair of sneakers.

We talk ourselves out of service all the time because it can seem as if issues are insurmountable. The world, the communities we love, are awash with challenges. It's only too easy to shrug and tell yourself nothing you do will make a difference. This is wrong.

Little things can mean everything. A bench to sit on. A field to play in. A hand to hold to know you aren't alone. Small moments can matter as much as big ones in the long run. You never know how your act of service will impact someone.

What I do know is that if you do nothing, you impact no one. And that's not why we're here.

I believe it's only by God's grace that I've been able to live this life, that I found basketball and secured my livelihood and sense of purpose. I believe just as steadfastly that the repayment of this divine debt is the service I give to others. I was given a chance. And so, in return, I wake up every morning with the intention to give others a chance, to be their ladder of hope.

It's something Carolyn Peck, the first Black coach to win

an NCAA women's national basketball championship, did for me after her victory with Purdue. She gifted me a piece of the championship net she cut down. Carolyn told me she wanted me to hold on to that piece of nylon until we earned our own national title. She suspected that I was close to winning it. Sometimes you need an edge to get you over the top.

I kept that piece of net in my wallet for years. That gesture of hers, it became a touchstone. The nylon was with me when South Carolina won the title in 2017. Carolyn called me after that victory and said, "Now go find the next coach you believe deserves a piece of the net."

I thought it over for a long while. Then months later while I was speaking with a reporter, he asked me what I was intending to do with our championship net and in the moment, I said, "I'm going to give pieces of it to every Black female Division I coach. Because they're looking at me and imagining their own futures."

I know it's unlikely all of them will win an NCAA championship. Giving them the token of the net was meant to light the torch of hope that had been lit for me. To pass it on.

I wanted those seventy-plus women to know I had their backs. If they were having a tough run, I wanted that piece of nylon to be there as a symbol of the good that comes from pushing through. Not every meaningful accomplishment needs to be a national championship. There are all types of wins that change lives in profound ways. Most of them don't come with trophies.

Ahead of the 1996 Olympics, Nike told me they were planning to do a mural with my likeness in Philly. One hundred feet tall, sixty-seven feet wide, smack dab in the middle of Center City, painted on a building at Eighth and Market Streets. When I heard, I was speechless. I viewed myself as an up-and-coming point guard who happened to be playing with iconic household names such as Lisa Leslie and Sheryl Swoopes. I occupied more of what I determined was a service role.

After I'd had several exploratory conversations with Nike, the powers that be there took a liking to me. Probably because I'm a sneakerhead. And because I was honest.

In all our chats, I stayed real. I didn't know whether that was the savvy play. Often in corporate America people say they want truthful conversations, but they really don't want you to say what's on your mind. With Nike, they asked for feedback. They wanted my unvarnished opinions. So, I gave them. I was up on shoes. Always have been. I told them I didn't really care what I looked like from my ankles up if ankles down my sneakers were nice and clean and cool.

It's part of what prompted Nike to later design for me a namesake shoe: the Nike Air Zoom S5. It launched during my first WNBA season in 1999. I'd asked the designers for a leather shoe that had a little shine to it, that was fly and not too girly. I didn't want my sneaker to look like a woman's shoe. I wanted everyone to respond to the aesthetic. I remember before they hit the market, I took a sample pair back to my neighborhood court to get some feedback. Nobody had a bad word to say.

When the Dawn Staley mural was announced, I learned I would be part of a club of nine prior Nike athletes to have public paintings, joining Charles Oakley in New York, Michael Jordan and Scottie Pippen in Chicago, Barry Sanders in Detroit, Jerry Rice in San Francisco, Cal Ripken in Baltimore, Mike Piazza in Los Angeles, and Mookie Blaylock in Atlanta. I was the first woman player they chose.

The image was of me running, ball in hand, dressed in my Team USA uniform. At the bottom were the words "Born in Philadelphia. Grew up on the corner of 25th and Diamond."

The unveiling was to be on April 12, 1996, when the national team was playing an exhibition game in Philadelphia. When I told my family about the mural and that they should come to the launch, I knew they didn't fully understand what it all meant. Hell, I didn't even fully understand what it meant. When I arrived, there were already more than two hundred spectators waiting. When I lifted my head and eyed the painting, I was floored. My image covered eight stories. I was larger than life. As tall as I felt inside.

My mom was arriving separately in another car. A southern woman, she did not drive. She didn't even have a driver's license. She took public transportation everywhere. Of course, if you were ever riding in a vehicle with her, she would still tell you exactly where to go.

I was already on the scene when she arrived. I watched her slowly walk up and catch sight of the mural, then burst into tears. She shook her head as if she couldn't believe it. To see her baby girl gracing a building that she'd passed from the seat of the bus every week for decades was nothing short of incredible.

I don't think my mom really knew how big an impact her daughter had made on the culture until that moment. It's one thing to see me hoop. Quite another to see me memorialized downtown like a civil rights leader or a pop star. Her unmistakable pride meant more to me than anything else that happened that day.

Like I said, I wasn't one of the famous players. I never chased the spotlight. But that mural was the exception that proved the rule. Being a hero in my hometown mattered to me.

In 2017, Philly designated Dawn Staley Lane, a two-block stretch that runs from my childhood home to the Hank Gathers Recreation Center—a path I walked probably a million times as a kid, ball in hand.

When all is said and done, I'm a six-time WNBA All-Star, a Hall of Famer, an Olympian, an Olympic coach, a two-time ABL All-Star, a two-time USA Basketball Female Athlete of the Year, the first person to win the prestigious Naismith Award as both a player and a coach, and the recipient of more accolades than I ever knew existed. But what I'm most proud of is being an odds beater.

Growing up where I did, I understood that people looking in from the outside believed I wasn't supposed to amount to anything. The odds were stacked against me. And I demolished them.

I view my life as a testimony of hope. Proof anyone can inspire, motivate, and improve the world around them. Anyone can become a ladder. All it takes is the will to do so. As I told the crowd on hand the day my mural was revealed, everything is out there waiting for you. You just have to start climbing.

It's Not Where You Start, It's Where You Finish

M y upbringing had taught me toughness, resilience, and that I could survive. But had it readied me to be a citizen of a place where most people did not look, think, or act like me? I was so comfortable in my corner of the world. And now that corner was fading fast in the rearview mirror.

The afternoon I left for college, I walked a lap of my neighborhood. I wanted to take it in, in its entirety, one final time before I moved away. I drank in the enormity of the towers. The sharply manicured lawns of our block. The pink zinnias my mother had planted. I nodded at the packs of kids hanging out, chatting and joking and trying to seem older than they were. I saw other teenagers shooting around, passing the ball back and forth, hustling for every point, the normal trash talk of our local games. I sensed that my leaving wouldn't change much. The ebb and flow of our tight-knit community would forge onward without me.

My eyes lingered on the basketball courts. I tried to picture myself at eight years old. The ball as big as my torso. Marching down to the court, confident that as much as any place on earth, that was the place for me.

I'd proven as much, many times over. But it hit me that day, what if I didn't live a stone's throw from a basketball court? I was not born into a family that held strong beliefs about the importance of a college education. My siblings and I were expected to finish high school and get good jobs. What if I never ventured out and trusted myself to know where I belonged?

I eventually learned North Philly would never be in the rearview. My hometown was as integral to me as my spine. I'm sure most people feel the same about their childhood homes. Good or bad, they shape you. They become the template for your future, the comparison for all that comes after. They say you can't go home again. But honestly, you don't need to. Home travels with you always. And nowhere is that truer than with North Philly.

As I would soon come to understand, being raised in Philadelphia, specifically in the Raymond Rosen projects, set me up to conquer the world and adversity in a way most other neighborhoods and cities never could. But that didn't mean moving elsewhere wouldn't be a challenge.

I'd managed my college recruiting process largely on my own. I didn't want to put my mom or dad out, so I interviewed with prospective schools myself. There was *a lot* of incoming interest. I'd graduated from Dobbins Tech in 1988 as the number one high school player in the country. We'd won three straight Philadelphia Public League championships. Every program came after me. Hundreds. I was fielding endless calls, listening to them make their pitch. This went on for years.

When it came down to deciding which university to attend, I cut right to the chase. I stayed loyal to the people who were with me from the beginning, who invested early when my talent was far from developed or guaranteed.

UVA had been recruiting me since eighth grade. As had Penn State. Those two schools ended up being the sole two campuses I visited.

To me, building a bond with my coach was paramount. Of all the potential suitors, I meshed most easily with Debbie Ryan at Virginia—a legend—as well as with Rene Portland, head coach at Penn State, and her assistant coach, Dan Durkin, whom I really respected.

After years of courtship and the in-person campus visits, I ultimately selected Virginia for a couple of reasons. One, I didn't want to go to a school that had already won a national championship. I wanted to be a part of building that legacy. The other deciding factor was the dorms. No joke.

I toured Penn State first. They showed me around the campus, which was fine. The players weren't very warm to me. They had a lot of guards. During my visit I felt the energy of "She's not coming here to take my spot."

Then they took me to the housing units. They were the old-fashioned layout where you share a pocket-sized room, and then for the bathroom, you walk down the hall. You're wearing your robe and slides, toting your bucket, your shower pail. I was like, okay, that ain't going to work.

I didn't know there was such a thing called a germaphobe back then, but I probably was one. Besides, I'd already lived in a household of seven people sharing one bathroom. I was due for a come up.

When you are a recruiter, you know that there are going to be some nonnegotiables. The nonnegotiable for me was accommodation. It was important for me to have my own space.

Now, on my official visit with Virginia, they showed me a residential suite. It was plush. It had a generous common area, two or three showers, three stalls per suite. Coming from the projects, I felt like I was moving into my own condo. The players were warmer, too. I was sold.

Sidenote: When I first got to South Carolina, we tried hard not to take parents and recruits to the dorm. When they'd ask to check them out, I'd wince. The setup wasn't great. Dated and, well, like Penn State back when I was recruited. Now, though, the housing at USC is incredible. We have mainly double suites, so it's just you and a roommate. There's a common area, a kitchen, *a washer and dryer*. We have a quad for four roommates, and we've noticed our freshmen want to live together. It's a great situation because it promotes off-court bonding. The location is a stone's throw from our practice facilities. I can look outside of my office window and see where our players live. It's a dream scenario for me and for the women who play for us.

When I was their age, the net result of my college campus explorations was that I just didn't feel it at Penn State. And maybe because of that, along with my being dazzled by the UVA dorms, I failed to notice other salient facts about the environment I was about to inhabit. Like, how freaking white it was.

I grew up surrounded by Black people. I didn't really interact with any white people until my later stages of playing AAU basketball. That's when I really got a sense of the divide in this country. Even in Philly, it was a tale of two cities.

My white teammates would marvel when they came to my neighborhood. They were curious. They'd come to check it out, like an urban field trip. Their parents wouldn't let them visit if it was dark. (If it was even close to dark.) Then they would drive me to their places in the suburbs, these large homes with ancient trees and lawns like parks, long driveways and brass knockers on the doors. I'd think, *Oh, this is how they live.* Their houses resembled something out of a television show. We were existing in two different worlds.

Those first months in Charlottesville I felt something similar. When I think back on my eighteen-year-old self, leaving North Philly and venturing to the great unknown of the University of Virginia, I recall a young woman filled with angst, unprepared, out of her element.

When I arrived, all I knew was North Philly and basketball. UVA was miles outside my comfort zone. The area was beautiful, breathtaking even. The fall so vibrant it reminded me of the puzzles I put together every Christmas. Picture-perfect. But the vibe was jarring.

I had no idea what I had gotten myself into. I didn't resemble or dress or talk like the folks I saw around me. I wasn't wise to the unspoken rules of a culture so removed from my own.

I struggled to adjust to an environment where I felt like an alien. It was like I was plucked from the grit of the projects and thrown into a pumpkin spice latte pool.

My solve was to fixate on my game. I didn't allow myself a social life. It wasn't a huge sacrifice. As I've said, I'm socially inept. Now, I was no odder in college than I was in high school, but walking onto the grounds (they made sure to call them that, "the grounds," never "campus") at the University of Virginia as a freshman, I definitely felt like I was.

Everyone on the grounds looked alike. Everyone seemed to have more money than I did. Everyone operated under an umbrella of catchphrases and commonalities that I had no reference for. I was a fish out of water, slowly suffocating.

I had the touchstone of basketball, thank goodness. I knew I would graduate college. What I didn't know, and what I didn't have the maturity to articulate at the time, was whether I'd be able to thrive in a community that wasn't North Philly.

Even if I had a good time around my teammates, I could count on one hand the number of times I ventured out. And only then because we had recruits on school visits. Half of the nights, I would still bail. Tell my teammates, "I'm not going, y'all can go."

It's so funny, Duke's associate head coach, Tia Jackson, gives me a hard time every time I see her on the recruiting trail. "I visited Virginia while you were playing there, and you didn't say a single thing to me." She says all I did was give her a nod, like, what's up? "I didn't pick UVA because you didn't talk to me. It's your fault!" she teases.

Today I know it was wrong of me not to extend myself.

I didn't do what my UVA teammates did for me on my campus visit. I wasn't mature enough to be welcoming or approachable. I would kill one of my players if they were as rude or absent as I was at their age. Oh, we would have a long talk. Back at UVA, though, I thought I was justified.

Why should I have to be the school's ambassador? My game was my message. I told myself that my time was better spent becoming a superior basketball player. I'd hole up in the dorm, watch ESPN. Review game tape. On loop. Like I was a detective searching for clues. It would be easy to say I didn't try to socialize because I was practicing unyielding devotion to my sport, but really, it suited my personality not to.

I didn't care that I was alone, or missing out. I wasn't open to making new friends. In Philly we stayed in our lanes. If I'm not comfortable with you, I'm not going to give you me.

Honestly, at the time, I considered many of the students I met silly and immature. They were sheltered. They lacked street sense. The towns and cities from which they came had not prepped them to be on their own. They weren't conditioned to be aware of their surroundings. Leaving a bike unlocked, expecting it to be there when they returned, I mean, *come on.* They'd leave their book bags unattended and go eat lunch. Asking for trouble. My classmates would say I was skeptical, distrustful, suspicious. Which was fine with me. I knew better than to run into a building when everyone else was running out. And, often, they didn't.

Thinking critically now as an adult, I saw that what they really were was unprepared. For the life of me, I could not understand how they missed glaring environmental and social cues; how they ambled gormlessly through their days without the intuition or instincts that came naturally to me.

Of course, at eighteen, I didn't recognize the survival mechanisms I'd developed in Philly as skills. In fact, I didn't recognize them at all. They were just an ingrained part of how I moved through the world. What I did grasp was how my spikier characteristics made me stand out as different. And the more different I felt, the spikier I became.

Have you ever had a difficult time being in the moment? When your mind wanders to different places and times, and you ruminate on days gone by or what could have been? That was me my opening semesters in college. I was miserable. I was chippy. I wanted to go home, and everyone knew it. It wasn't anything I had to verbalize; it was obvious in my behavior.

I shuffled through *the grounds* with my head down, eschewing eye contact with anyone who passed by. I hid in my room. I was largely mute. My only bright spot was playing ball. If I could have stayed in the gym all day, I would have.

Unfortunately, in college, they expect you to attend class. I went, but I was uncomfortable every day. Unfocused. At best a mediocre student, I wasn't prepared for the academic rigors of UVA. As far as I was concerned, I was there to play ball. Academics were a means to an end.

I found myself gravitating less to school and seeking out local courts throughout Charlottesville. I went where the townies played. The games on those outdoor courts weren't as hardcore as those I'd played in the projects, but I got to mix it up with the guys. The looser, harder style reminded me of home. I guess I was trying to replicate what I had back in Philly. The rough-and-tumble outdoor games that raised me. A place where I understood the rules.

My attitude and detachment began to show up in my grades. Neglecting my studies and social life had put my basketball scholarship in jeopardy. It was only my first year, and they were contemplating kicking me out. Before long, I was summoned to the dean's office.

Understand, I'm nineteen years old, drowning in anxiety, itchy in my skin in every way. There was less than a snowball's chance in hell this come-to-Jesus was going to go well. I walked into my sit-down with the dean and made no eye contact. Not an auspicious beginning when you're trying to convince someone to keep you around.

Now, Coach Debbie Ryan probably set the stage ahead of time. I'm sure she warned the dean I wasn't the best communicator off the court. Gave my background. I was terminally shy! But a once-in-a-generation point guard! My job was to charm and connect with the dean, be the closer, and persuade the school I should not be dismissed. But instead, like clockwork, North Philly showed up.

After a few introductory niceties, the dean gave me a once-over, then said, "You're going to have to start conforming to the way we do things here at Virginia."

Conform?

If it were a movie, this would've been where you'd hear the needle-scratch sound effect.

In my head, my monologue was like, *I'm not conforming. I'm not kissing nobody's ass. And certainly not the asses of these preppy white people, these elitist jerks. No, I'm going to be myself. Always. So yeah, this is me. Take it or leave it.*

My white-hot reaction was set off by that one word. *Conform.* My interior dialogue was all fiery Philly talk. While my exterior communication was ice-cold crossed arms and cutting eyes.

In the moment, I wasn't getting it. I'd dug myself a hole, with no clear escape. There I was, allegedly fighting for my scholarship and future as a player, and I was allowing one word to pull the pin on my emotional grenade. I know this now as an adult. But in that room, I doubled down on attitude.

Now, I will say, and I know this as a coach, sometimes word choice is everything to young people. If instead of "conform," the dean had said "pivot" or "adjust," maybe I would have received the message. But this was 1989. Coaches and deans and ADs weren't amending their vernacular to avoid offending kids. It was a different time. Nobody cared if you were insulted or hurt.

I exited the dean's office without saying two words. I didn't fall on my sword. I didn't have that in me at the time. I resentfully listened. Then I left.

Debbie had to go back and do cleanup. She probably needed a hazmat suit. She begged the dean: "I hear you, but we need to keep her."

Debbie had been head coach at Virginia since 1977, back when money for women's sports was what you dug out of your couch cushions. In those days, female players often didn't even have their own locker rooms. Or bathrooms. They had to use the men's or make do. Uniforms, equipment, all of it was hand-me-down. Women's teams traveled by bus, players washed their own jerseys. All to say, Debbie was used to fighting hard fights.

When you're young, you don't know what you don't know. I was ignorant—incredibly ignorant, to be honest. I wasn't thinking about the context of all that came before me. Or what I was risking by being willful. I needed a wake-up call.

It made me think back to when I was young and had a boyfriend who was monopolizing my time. I called him Boodles. Vincent was his real name. We spent hours gabbing on the phone. I'm a rules follower. I do what I'm supposed to do, but because of Boodles, I did not study for this one science test.

On the day of the exam, I knew I couldn't pass. So, I cheated. Badly. My cheat sheet was an eight-by-eleven sheet of paper. I slid it right behind the test. Genius plan, right?

My teacher, Mr. Polowski, clocked me immediately. I was not slick. I probably looked unprepared and guilty on top of that. He quietly walked up to my desk, picked up my test, and revealed the biggest cheat sheet in history. He then took both pieces of paper and silently returned to the front of the class, leaving me to marinate in my bad choices. It was worse than getting yelled at. It was humiliating.

I had that sinking feeling you have when you've shown your butt in front of your peers. I was sinking in my chair, sweating, thinking about my mother's embarrassment when Mr. Polowski would tell her of my moral failings. I knew what I'd done was a terrible representation of who I was and what my family, what my parents, especially, expected from me.

Needless to say, after that I got my act together at school. I wasn't going to permit anything or anyone to distract me from my goals. Boodles took a back seat. I woke up.

At Virginia, my wake-up call was coming from inside the house. After I had a chance to process my meeting with the dean and the severity of what she'd threatened, something stirred in me. I digested the risk to my goals at hand. If I didn't change, I wouldn't be able to remain in the game. My eligibility would be revoked. I realized I had to "play ball" to play ball.

In the end, wrong language or not, I needed to hear that message, because I was not going back home to North Philly a dropout. I knew better than to toss my ambitions away for pride or let my shyness and obstinance derail my dreams. I wasn't going to beat myself.

I pulled my shoulders back, took a deep breath, and returned to what I knew would motivate me: competition. I flipped my staying on at UVA into a way of competing against the dean. I made my grades about competing with my classmates. Just like with basketball, when I'm challenged, I'm better. I'll do whatever I need to do to win. I knew if I was going to survive at UVA, I needed to deliberately alter my habits. This was an uncomfortable realization and an even more uncomfortable process. But it was grow or fold. I wasn't folding.

It's not where you start, it's where you finish.

I clicked the television off. I went easier on my peers. I learned the UVA fight song. I ventured out to a football game and was swept up in the student camaraderie. I let my friends get me drunk. Once! Orange juice and vodka. I went hard. If I was drinking, I wasn't going to sit there and babysit it. The next day we had an away game. I was sick as all get-out. That was the end of the drinking.

I swallowed my pride on the court as well. That was a heavier lift.

I'm an instinctual player. I had talent, flair. I could do flashy things with my passing. I scored and made steals. But I didn't necessarily value the ball. In my freshman year, I averaged five turnovers a game. Embarrassing.

UVA was a learning curve for me because I hadn't had basketball broken down into fundamentals before college. I thought it was meaningless. The methodology didn't make sense in my mind. I wanted to roll the ball out. Let's go.

Debbie used drills to get me to stop and think. And to foster team communication. I recall one drill we did once, where a player would hold the ball up and you'd snatch it, then call ball or rebound. I was uncomfortable speaking up, so I'd jump and grab that ball, higher than everybody on the team, but I wouldn't say anything.

Debbie would prod me, "Open your mouth." I'd ignore her or mumble under my breath. I have such empathy for her now. It was a nightmare case of your star player not doing what they're supposed to do. In front of the whole team.

As starting point guard, being vocal is essential. Debbie utilized the drills, but she also forged a personal relationship with me that made me feel safe enough to try new things. She teased me about my height. (She's short, too.) She knew I responded to humor. She deciphered my personality and trusted that if she gave me enough independence, I would come to where she needed me to be. Debbie was a smart cookie.

When I was flailing, she stayed cool, let me play through mistakes. Debbie's approach was not to hector me and say, "Don't turn over the ball!" She flagged areas to adjust but then let me unpack and address the flaws on my own.

It was under Debbie's coaching that I incorporated the tool of snapping a rubber band on my wrist. I would wear an elastic and if I turned the ball over, I would snap myself. (I borrowed the technique from the great Mo Cheeks.) The self-imposed adversity training worked great. My turnover ratio fell.

Debbie's approach was to let me be me. In a funny way, allowing me to commit repeated turnovers made me sicker sooner of fumbling the ball. She knew if she forced her will on me, I wouldn't be as effective.

Every coach I've had has utilized different tactics. Debbie wanted to win as much as any of them. But she coached all her players as individuals. She invested in who we were as people and gave us space to make a few messes. She knew we were like any other young women at that stage of life: where we started was not where we'd end up. She also knew there was more to life than basketball.

Debbie would tell anyone who asked that coaching was not about the wins and losses. Wins are great in the moment. But what her players did once basketball was behind them was the crux of why she coached. For her, knowing she was an important part of somebody's life, for the rest of their life, was the point. After being a coach myself all these years, I can't say I disagree.

Debbie was truly the best coach for me in that emergent period of my career because she knew how I was wired. That all I wanted to do was to improve and be the best, and no one would motivate me more than I would.

Debbie trusted that I was going to be a smarter decision maker if she let me actually make the decisions, rather than being told what to do. All of which served to make me a much finer point guard.

Over time, I noticed when I spoke up, my Virginia teammates leaned in. I could tell they were eager to hear what I had to say even if I was timid about saying it. The more I communicated, the more we clicked, the more we executed, the more we won. The math was clear. Now, when it came time to speak to the media, I'd still make myself scarce. Debbie says I would literally hide. That I speak to the press almost daily now is testament to the fact that change is possible, and even the wariest, quietest, most insecure of us can find our voice.

My progress wasn't a straight line. It took a lot of patience from Debbie to get me through. After a first-round game in the ACC tournament, Debbie and I exchanged heated words. She'd been my advocate. Putting herself on the hook on my behalf. Now it was my turn to get with the program.

Debbie was frustrated by my stubbornness and impatience with, well, everything. A part of me still believed I knew best. Debbie told me I was a transformative player. That I knew how to control the game from any position. If needed, I was there, scoring, rebounding, taking the temperature of whom I could pass to. But! She reminded me, despite my best efforts, I could not win a championship alone.

The time had come for me to learn that the value of teamwork is greater than the sum of individual ambitions.

Like I said, Debbie was a smart cookie. She cared about her players and what became of us after we left UVA. I know Debbie called on me to develop and grow as a point guard because she knew I would also grow as a person.

After my first year, my mother phoned Debbie. When Coach answered, my mom asked her, "What did you do to my daughter?" Concerned, Debbie questioned, "What do you mean?" And my mom shot back with a laugh, "She came home talking!"

My mother was surprised to see how in just one year, I'd already grown up so much. With a fair amount of prodding, I'd come ever so slightly out of my shell. I'd met folks halfway. Taught myself I could change. Realized everything I thought I knew about life, about basketball, wasn't all there was to be known. My college experience was doing exactly as it advertised. It was expanding my horizons.

The truth is, the stories you tell yourself can be as harmful as anything that anyone else says about you. I'd arrived at school convinced I was a certain type of player, a certain type of person. Streetwise. Tough. No bullshit. What I'd done to that point—played hard and stayed in my lane—had worked. Why would I change? Thanks to Debbie, the assistant coaching staff, the college dean, my teammates, my classmates, and my own internal voice, I looked in the mirror and concluded I could do better by being better.

The good news about transformation is that it's infectious. I remember during scrimmages, Debbie divided us into teams of starters and teams of nonstarters, plus me. I would be placed with the players who didn't get much court action. And yet, my team never lost a scrimmage. Not one in four years.

My burgeoning confidence helped fuel our runs, but our collective focus sealed the victory. It proved to me that any group focused on the same result, giving maximum effort, will win every time. No matter that our team weren't the starters. We became the finishers.

I came into UVA sure my best asset was mental toughness. Growing up playing with boys, I had to throw down that much harder. In high school, the game wasn't as closely regulated. The rules looser. In college basketball, the rules were the rules, the stakes exponentially higher. Virginia was the first time I was really stressed on the court. Coaches feed their families off wins. Universities obtain revenue from success. The pressure inevitably trickles down to the players.

I was resilient. But I had to teach myself how to control my emotions, to be unflappable in tense moments. Time and time again it was my responsibility to make the last play, or to take the final shot. My team followed my lead. If I unraveled or choked, so would they.

By my fourth and final year, I was seasoned enough that I could go to the free throw line with the win in the balance and completely shut out thousands of screaming fans with ease. I'd learned to maintain intensity, but in a composed way.

Then came the night in 1992 when we played Stanford in the Final Four.

It's burned in my memory. The last game of my college career. Barreling toward the national championship victory

I'd been fantasizing about since I was in grade school. We entered the tourney ranked number one.

While I was at UVA, we'd made it to the Final Four three consecutive times.

Our first run had ended in 1990 with a 66–75 loss to Stanford. Our second defeat was in the finals to Tennessee. We lost in overtime, 67–70. I'd scored twenty-eight points and became the only player from a losing team to be honored as the Final Four's Most Outstanding Player, but I was still crushed. I lived with that loss all year until our third at bat. And here we were, three Final Fours later, up against Stanford, déjà vu all over again.

We opened strong and held the lead most of the game. With eight minutes to go, we were ahead 51–44. We kept saying, we need to put this to bed. But Stanford would not go down easy. Cardinal guard Kate Paye was on me like lint on velvet. I could not brush her off. She kept my scoring down to six points in the final seven minutes as Stanford rallied from deficits four times in a row, guard Molly Goodenbour sinking threes to tie the game, then inch ahead.

The last possession, Stanford shot the ball. It flew out of bounds with time remaining, but the refs gestured the arm signal for game over. As they left the court, I sprinted behind them and yelled, "There's still time on the clock!"

They looked shocked, but after a huddle and review, the officials determined I was right. As they were trying to figure out how much time would be added back, Debbie gathered us to diagram a miracle play. The plan was for me to receive the ball for a quick catch and shoot.

The game clock was restarted with .08 seconds to go. Plenty of time.

We ran the play. I caught the inbound pass, turned, bounced the ball once, took my shot. And . . . it fell short.

In front of a crowd of more than twelve thousand, my twenty-six-footer bounced off the glass and fell to the floor. Stanford had won by a single point, 66–65.

In the moment, my spirit collapsed. I couldn't process that we didn't win. That the achievement I'd spent my whole life training for was never going to be mine. No trophy. No parade. No confetti falling from the sky.

It was the last time I'd don my UVA uniform. There were no more chances. I'd be graduating college without a national championship.

"I can't believe this is over," I wailed, weeping. Debbie was crying, too. "We had the shots," she told the press. "They just didn't go in."

As the game wrapped, I did my best to hold my head high and look each opponent in the eye as we hurriedly shook hands. Once I was alone, the tears flowed again, fast and furious.

Not long after that defeat, I graduated with a degree in rhetoric and communication studies and left UVA. I exited the NCAA as the all-time steals leader and having scored 2,135 points. From 1990 through 1992, our team record was 92–11. I was twice awarded National Player of the Year. My goal of becoming an Olympian was firmly on the horizon. All achievements to be proud of.

And yet part of me couldn't shake the grief of losing our shot at the NCAA title. I carried the shadow of it until South

Carolina, where I lived through what Debbie had been expressing while I was at UVA. The true joy of coaching. Being a dream merchant for others.

Those years at Virginia had changed me. When I left, I was no longer the all-Philly-all-the-time hard-ass among a sea of strangers. Every step of the journey, every battle with my coaches, my classmates, the emotional turmoil, the psychological obstacles, I needed.

I was young. I couldn't see the big picture at the time. But I do now.

Once the regret of the title loss faded some, I came to appreciate that although I had been recognized for my accomplishments on the court, the greater reward came from being a part of the team. And my greatest reward remained a mystery still to come. The future was unwritten.

We all fail, all the time. Genius once-in-a-generation players fail all the time. Great leaders fail all the time. Pros fail all the time. The solution is to go home, take stock, press yourself on what you can do better, and try again. A loss reminds you what your standards are.

When I became a coach, I implemented a "twenty-four-hour rule." We lose, we mess up, the clock starts ticking. You're allowed to pout or moan for twenty-four hours before moving on. Same for the wins. Celebrate, feel your oats. Then get your head back in the game.

The theory of the case is this: It's not about where you start. It's about where you finish. And the finish line isn't always where you think it is. (Spoiler alert—the one true finish line isn't in your control anyway.)

I've kept that philosophy front and center my whole career since leaving college. Admittedly, it isn't the easiest advice to follow. I struggled mightily when our South Carolina team lost to Iowa in the 2023 Final Four.

That defeat rocked me. I couldn't understand. We had a team full of players who did all the right things. You're not supposed to ask, why does this happen? You're not supposed to question God. But we're human and we want to know, what's the reason? Why would the universe do that? Why would you leave us here?

I wasn't asking for me. I wanted to know for my players. That team as a unit, they were the best to be around. They did exactly what was needed, no questions asked. If you knew this group of young ladies, you'd want them to win.

Then we traveled all the way to the Final Four, undefeated. And bam! The happy ending of the fairy tale was snatched away, just as it had been for me at Virginia.

Part of my pain was, damn, I'll never get to coach this team again. These players who've given so much. I don't recall what I said to them after the game. Probably that I didn't know what the meaning was behind this loss, but basketball's been great to us, and we should be thankful for the victories and the defeats.

People reading this book may say, well, Caitlin Clark, that's what brought the hammer, the heartache. The end of the road for our dazzling "freshies" class one game shy of a chance to win back-to-back NCAA titles. Believe me when I tell you it wasn't losing on the court with Clark that hurt. We could have lost to the Little Sisters of the Poor and felt the same way.

What any leader must reckon with is that there's not a whole lot of opportunity to strengthen your mentality without failure. The secret is not to think about what you've lost, but about what you can gain. Don't let adversity define you. Let it build you. Like the song says, Mama said there'd be days like this. And mine certainly did. My mother expected me to fight on. Rolling over and giving up was not an option for her and as such it was not one for me either.

The reality is that there's only ever going to be one winner. Everybody else is the loser. You're in good company. The deeper anguish comes when the reason you lost was avoidable. That's a harder pill to swallow. At the levels we're playing, the margin of error is that tiny.

As a rule, I don't get rattled. If our opponent goes on a 10–0 run, most coaches get panicky. I don't flinch. A 10–0 run doesn't mean that you're not taking good shots. It doesn't mean you aren't defending the run. If you are, eventually the shots will fall, and the game will balance itself. I don't get caught up in the scoreboard. Are we in our right defensive stance? Are we making tactical decisions? If so, it's going to work out.

That philosophy applies to the wider frame of a season, a legacy, a life. Careers are long. Life is long. Perspective is key. Before you know it, that missed layup, or clumsy turnover, even the loss of a title will be a distant memory. Success is all about being able to bounce back.

A year after we lost to Iowa, our Gamecocks went unde-, feated with the most unlikely team. Wilder, sillier. I would joke that coaching them was like running a day care. (After I made that analogy to the press, a company even made T-shirts that said "Dawn's Day Care.") The players would act young and foolish, and I'd sigh and tell myself I should have retired last season.

But then, as we persisted, the team gelled. They kind of fell in love with each other and were driven by the desire not to let each other down. Being written off as underdogs can motivate like nothing else. We ended a perfect season (the tenth Division I team to do so) with an 87–75 victory over the Hawkeyes for the championship title.

We made history. Winning in front of a record viewership of 18.7 million, the most-watched basketball game, men's or women's, pro or college, since 2019. Players from the former heartbreak season were there, weeping like they won.

That's what I call uncommon favor.

The spiritual messaging to me was clear. You may have lost that one championship. The one you thought you deserved. Now watch what I do. I'm going to get you all the way to that same point, a place you thought that you would never get back to. And I'm going to do it with a team that lost six of its top players. A team you underestimated. You're going to prevail in spite of all that. And now you're going to believe me when I tell you I'm alive and well in your life.

It felt like a test of faith that I had to take and pass. Like I said during my postgame interview with ESPN, "God has a funny way of dealing with people."

That astonishing journey made me believe a bit deeper. When you're at your worst and your weakest moments, God's at his best. It made me reexamine losing, too. How much you can gain from loss.

I lost at Virginia. I lost at South Carolina. I've lost more times than I can count. I know now that every loss strengthens me for whatever I'm going to face in the future. The losses remind me that what feels like an end can be a beginning.

You Have to Do What You Don't Want to Do to Get What You Want

When I graduated from the University of Virginia in May 1992, I was inside a cloud of uncertainty. I'd been named college basketball's player of the year for the second time. I'd signed with an agent, Bruce Levy, who was promising to get me on an international team. Bruce, who had run his own agency since 1979, had a lock on all the female players coming out of college. He was the first real agent for women's professional basketball. But for all of Bruce's efforts and my optimism and expectation, it wasn't happening.

The leagues overseas limited the number of foreigners per team. I knew a few other players were headed to Europe in September and October, but none of the squads there needed guards. Guards were a dime a dozen. The foreign teams wanted post players, and they wanted players with hype. And player of the year or not, I was low on the hype meter.

I left Charlottesville and headed home to Philly. I had nowhere else to go.

Like most serious athletes back then, I never went to school for a degree per se. I went to play basketball. Now as a coach, as a leader of young women, I try to mentor about real life. Explain to them that not everyone can play ball forever. But that was not my thinking when I was a recent graduate. So, I went to Philly and waited for the call.

My mother was cleaning houses at the time. She worked for a man who owned a retail store and asked him whether he could provide me with a job. My mom was forever getting jobs for all us kids through her cleaning clients. The man agreed to hire me and assigned me to the floor, where I was to greet customers and fold clothes. I was terrible. I mean, I was fine at folding, but I used to run from the customers because I didn't care to interact with strangers. I'd matured in college, but I hadn't had a personality transplant. My direct report started giving me a hard time. Not for the crappy customer service, but because she thought I was there to take her job. I was like, "Lady, I don't want *this* job. Let alone yours."

After a few weeks I got my first paycheck. It was a couple hundred dollars. I remember thinking, *What am I supposed to do with that?* I was one of the best basketball players in the world, and here I was stuck stacking jeans, instead of playing the game I'd excelled at and been a part of for a decade.

Such was the case for the majority of women athletes after graduating from their college teams. Our opportunities were limited. There was no WNBA. My male counterpart who was the men's 1992 college player of the year had signed an NBA deal for $80 million. I was folding shirts for a couple hundred bucks.

After that initial paycheck and the obvious reality that customer service was not the career for me, I became even more determined to play basketball for a living. There wouldn't be any female pro leagues for five more years. I needed to play abroad or die trying.

The international gig was about more than money for me. A few months prior I'd gone to the Olympic training center to compete for a position on the 1992 women's basketball team. I was up against players who'd already been pros overseas, established names such as Teresa Edwards, Cynthia Cooper, Teresa Weatherspoon. Nonetheless, I was twenty-two and ready, coming off a dominant run at UVA.

When the day came to read the final roster for Barcelona, they brought each player before the decision-making committee members one by one. Walking in, I was certain I was a lock. I'd performed well in training. My record as a point guard was stellar. I waltzed in confidently wearing my Team USA basketball gear—only to be informed, in no short order, that I'd been cut.

I was stunned. I'd never failed that badly. My rattled response to the rejection was not a shining moment. I accused the committee of being political. Going with friends over ability. Or whatever I thought at the time.

The Olympic trials committee had provided two reasons why I didn't make the team. One: I was too short. And two:

I didn't have enough international experience. I couldn't do anything about my height. But I could go overseas.

As often happened when I was younger, as soon as I calmed down, I could think more clearly. Okay, getting passed over was a shock. What are my options now? I was at a cross-roads.

Do I give up? Never try out again? No effing way.

Do I put myself in a position where I'm going to be undeni-able next time? Abso-effing-lutely.

While I waited for a position to open, I resolved to pull myself together. I purged my anger, changed my internal con-versation. I stopped blaming other people. As my mom taught me, blaming others never solves anything anyway. It only gives them more power over you.

I considered that my not making the team was about more than just the physical piece. I lacked mental stamina. Maturity. Usefully, getting past the catastrophe of not being able to do the one thing that you worked toward your whole life tends to build psychological strength.

Besides, I lived to prove people wrong. I had a chip on my shoulder. When needed, that chip could act as rocket fuel.

That summer, I watched the US women's team compete in Barcelona and end up settling for bronze. Even from afar, I shared their frustration. I wished I could have been there, of course, but more than that, I wanted America to win. I re-committed to my scheme to be on the Olympic team next time. How I was going to get there with no formal training regimen, no coach, no access to the internal politics of the decision-making was a question I needed to answer.

Until I could answer, I played basketball multiple hours a day, any time of day. I kept my body competition-ready. Mentally, I counted on my past success to see me through. I was an invisible kid from the projects who'd made it to three NCAA national championships. I could claw my way onto Team USA.

After five months, my agent finally received an offer. There was an opening to play in Spain. As quickly as I could, I signed the contract for five thousand dollars a month and headed to hoop in Segovia. Adios, retail job.

I ended up playing abroad for three years. A trio of Olympic gold medals later, I felt pretty solid about my choice to have left the United States, but when I initially arrived in Segovia, I was adrift and homesick. Heading overseas is nothing like how it is now.

We had no access to the internet. The language barrier left me with few folks to talk to. I had a roommate, Dolores Bootz, and some teammates who spoke English. But that was it. I taught myself how to drive a stick shift just so I could drive the hour to Madrid to hang out with another American, Rhonda Mapp.

I found it hard to build a local community. I was shy. I didn't speak the language. I racked up two thousand dollars in phone bills because I missed my family and friends. I was in such denial about how long I'd be away that I never unpacked. I lived out of my suitcase. I would wash my clothes, fold them, and stow them back in the luggage like it was my dresser.

One plus was that I was grateful it was warmer in Spain than in Philly. But the food wasn't familiar. Or appealing to me. Everything closed down in the afternoon. Nothing like the

24/7 pace and convenience of American cities. Even figuring out basic errands in another language was challenging. On top of all that, I found myself alone during holidays.

Psychologically, I did all I could to make it work, trying to stay optimistic, reminding myself of my why—to make the Olympic team! But eventually I had to admit, I hated it abroad. I wanted to go home.

Then one afternoon in my room I was watching *House Party*. Movies one, two, and three. The whole trilogy on VCR. We were given a day off a week, and that day my big plan was to spend it with Kid 'n Play.

There was a scene in one of the films where Kid 'n Play were partying and messing around, and a professor catches them and reads them the riot act. As he's schooling them, the professor concludes his lecture, saying sternly, "You have to do what you don't want to do to get what you want."

My brain froze when I heard that line. I was like, *Ohhhh*. That's why I'm here. That message wasn't for you, Kid 'n Play. That message was for me.

You have to do what you don't want to do to get what you want.

I learned my life motto in that Spanish apartment. From a Kid 'n Play movie, of all places. I guess you never know who a messenger is going to be.

After that, I sucked it up. I wasn't going to bail on Europe. To be an Olympian, I needed to stay. I may as well enjoy what I could about the ride. Which I did, for the next three years over my multiple stints overseas. I'd bounce around teams, replace players when they got injured or cut, like a substitute teacher.

In 1994, I heard I'd made the senior team for the world championship. It was good to be back in the auspices of USA basketball, but our team was upset by Brazil in the semifinals. We settled for a bronze medal, just as we did in Barcelona.

Considered together, that wasn't a good look for the women of USA Basketball. There'd been a string of third-place finishes: at the 1994 world championships, the 1992 Olympics, and the 1991 Pan American Games. As a result, in 1995, the NBA decided to finance a traveling women's team that would tour the world in preparation for the 1996 Atlanta Games. By then I was playing in France, for a coach who is now the federation president for the French national team, John Pierre. (We called him "shay-pee," like "JP" with a terrible French accent.)

I was doing well in France, piling up international experience, honing my mental game. But with USA Basketball heading into their next team tryouts, the time had come. I booked a flight home.

Auditioning for Team USA is by invite only. I'm proud to say I was, along with thirty other basketball players, asked to the Colorado Springs Olympic Training Center for a weeklong trial. What we were trying out for was a chance to be a part of the historical USA Basketball women's national team. For you to make the Olympic team, you had to go through the national team first. We wouldn't hear about who made the Olympic squad until six to eight weeks prior to the Games.

At the training center, we played and played and played and played and played. Double sessions, or two-a-days. Remember, the altitude is something fierce in Colorado Springs.

It was survival of the fittest. I mean, we were balling, we were tired, we were balling, we were tired, we were balling. That was on repeat. What I remember most about the whole process is being wiped out. I felt like a dishrag in a dirty bucket.

My teammates, among them Lisa Leslie, Teresa Edwards, Katrina McClain, Carla McGhee, the late great Nikki McCray, Ruthie Bolton, Jennifer Azzi, Katy Steding, Sheryl Swoopes, and Rebecca Lobo (the only college player who was invited to the Olympic trials), fought to remain up to the task.

The committee wanted the perfect blend of players. They were testing us to make sure we had chemistry along with the fortitude to withstand the rigors of what we were about to venture into. After those first seven days, they made cuts. If you were one of the lucky ones who survived the week, your reward was more pain and suffering.

Stanford's coach, Tara VanDerveer, was there monitoring the process. Her priority was high-percentage basketball. Tara didn't tolerate a single mistake from anyone. (More on that later.)

After I was cut from the 1992 Olympic team and parked on the B team, Tara (who was part of USA Basketball) would often sidle up and ask, "If the Olympic coach wanted a point guard, do you think I should recommend you?"

I'd exclaim, "Yes! Of course. Why wouldn't you?"

Tara would listen to my pitch, then shake her head and say, "Nah. You turn the ball over too much."

At the time, that hurt my feelings. I mean, it stung. But she gave it to me strong. That part I appreciated.

I knew that I'd made the national team when at the end of

the second week they told me I was good, *thus far*, and offered me fifty thousand dollars to train for one year prior to the 1996 Games. Now, in most cases, fifty grand was well worth forgoing your international gigs. But players such as Teresa Edwards and Katrina McClain were making probably six figures at that point. To be a part of this historical national team meant that they would have to take a pay cut. I, however, looked at it as a come-up. To say nothing of my second chance at making it to the Olympics. I wanted to prove dreams delayed are not dreams denied.

They sent those of us who survived the culling home to recover and "enjoy the rest of the summer off." I say that with a whole shaker of salt. We went home, all right, but our newly appointed head coach, Tara VanDerveer, made sure the grueling workouts and brutal regimen followed us there in the mail.

The requirements were rigorous. Twelve weeks, six days a week. Monday, Wednesday, Friday we had cardio. You could take a class, like an aerobics class, but you had to do sixty minutes. If the class was fifty-five minutes and you reported you were five minutes short of the hour-long goal, that was not okay. We had to run three miles a day. We had to lift weights. When you were done with your week, you had to mail Tara the log. The paperwork had to be postmarked on Monday. If it was not postmarked by Monday, Tara would be none too pleased.

I'm a rules follower. You have to do what you don't want to do to get what you want. So, I followed all the instructions. Which set me up for success with Tara. When we reconvened at the national team training camp in the fall, we had a team meeting. We were given notebooks, and inside them Tara had recorded plays, her expectations, and the rules moving forward. She'd also transcribed the results of our summer workouts. That was when a lot of the team realized there was going to be a price to pay for not having executed Tara's summer to-do list to her exact specifications.

Every player who reported a minute short of the goal, a block short of a run, who didn't complete or turn in workouts or have them postmarked by the right date, was made a part of what was called the Breakfast Club.

I don't know exactly how many people were in the Breakfast Club. I know that I wasn't! Lisa wasn't either. I'm pretty sure Carla McGhee and Nikki McCray and all those Tennessee alums were. Any player in the Breakfast Club had to work out *prior* to our practices. Basically, two workouts in a row.

I really felt sorry for them because our practices were excruciating. We were already doing two-a-days. And the Breakfast Club had to log *three*. It sucked to be them at that point.

Tara was a perfectionist, and she wanted you to play without error. Practices were designed to lead us to that infallibility. Anything that felt off to her we had to repeat until we got it right. If we didn't, we had to run sprints.

Tara's approach hewed to what she did as a coach at Stanford. Her teams were always in great condition. She never wanted to worry about her players fatiguing in games.

To ready us for the Atlanta Games, Tara pushed us to physical and mental fatigue. It was the most draining time of my life. There would be no scenario in game play that Tara hadn't already tested or conditioned us for. So, she ran us. She ran us into the ground. However, I have to admit, once you got to that place, you had stamina.

Our team was a mixture of relative newbies and seasoned veterans. In my opinion, our veterans were picked on. Tara would mutter things like "You can't teach an old dog new tricks." Certain players were going into their third or fourth Olympic Games. They'd been a part of history. But as far as Tara was concerned, that wasn't necessarily a good thing.

On the flip side, our youngest player, Rebecca, also didn't have a chance. Tara treated her like the redheaded stepchild. I knew Rebecca internalized how Tara was painting her, as too junior, as immature. It's almost impossible not to take on how your coach sees you, especially in an environment as heightened as the one we were living through.

I felt bad on their behalf. The rest of the team did what we could to protect the singled-out players from Tara's wrath. Thankfully, we had some cool national team assistant coaches in Renee Brown and Nell Fortner. They were the best coaches we could have wished for in this situation, because for every unbearable thing Tara did, we were equally comforted by Renee and Nell.

It was very much bad cop, good cop. They would check the temperature of the room and the practices. They could defuse the angst and the tension, handle all the drama that came with what was an intense atmosphere. They kept us sane.

This was no small feat, as there was no letup. When we weren't practicing, we were on university tours. We visited every national team member's college. We traveled the country and the world, scrimmaging teams in preparation for Atlanta. There were zero hours that weren't filled.

Off the court, we had epic film sessions. Tara wanted us to comprehend why certain dynamics were happening out on the floor. She demanded all of us play flawless basketball from the jump, whether we knew her system or not. That paradigm was challenging for me because I'm a risk-taker.

On the court, everything was a competition. We literally had to pace ourselves. For instance, if Tara was paying attention down one end, and Teresa Edwards and I were at the other end, I would say, "Hey, she's not looking. Are you good, you good?" And the second Tara turned her attention back to us, we'd go. It was like sneaking behind the teacher's back.

Tara would correct every single thing. She would nag. Relentlessly criticize. She kept us on our toes, saying, "This is only the national team. The Olympic team isn't picked." She made sure she mentioned that all the time. Even when training was halfway done, she'd warn us that our positions weren't secure. It didn't feel like bluffing until the end. We'd spent nine months together. At a certain point, we were thinking, *Who else are you going to get at this point?*

Tara's style of coaching was calculating, methodical, manipulative even. At any given time, it was somebody's day. Well, not Ruthie. We all knew Ruthie was Tara's favorite. Ruthie was military. Tara was drawn to Ruthie's discipline and instinct to do what Tara told her to without any pushback. Ruthie followed the chain of command. She did her job with no extra guff. It was just, "Yes, ma'am."

If you weren't Ruthie, Tara would pick on you. She would

play mind games. She would mentally challenge you. Almost to the breaking point. Since we knew it was coming, we would all be prepared. Hey, Nik, it's your day. Hey, Dawn, it's your day. T, every day is your day. But especially today.

Tara knew what she wanted. How she went about getting it was very different from what we hoped for, but it was her way, and we were stuck with it.

We adapted. We were strong-minded individuals. We came from storied programs. We had played overseas. We were used to doing things the hard way. We weren't expecting the training to be a walk in the park. That said, Tara took it to a place she didn't need to, because we were such pros. It wasn't necessary to push us. We already had track records of pushing ourselves.

You have to do what you don't want to do to get what you want.

As you can imagine, Tara was practically despised. I don't know whether this was intentional or not. A subversive coaching technique. Either way, she didn't care. She was charged to do a job, she was going to do it her way, and her way might have been to get us to like each other more than we liked her. Well, I tell you, mission accomplished.

Even in the middle of all that maltreatment, I still retained some empathy for Tara. Team USA missed out on gold in 1992. All eyes were going to be on us in Atlanta. Tara was hell-bent on winning. There could be no third- or second-place finish this time.

On top of that, she was saddled with heading up a new Team USA policy, something that had never been done before, which was pulling the team together a year before the competition and designing a traveling road show. Tara had acute additional pressure not to let that experiment fail. Because the stakes there were far bigger than any Olympic Games. They were the trial balloon for the viability of the entire future of professional women's basketball.

We knew we were the guinea pigs. That the success of the 1996 "Women's Dream Team" in the Olympic Games would directly affect whether we got women's US professional basketball off the ground. We talked about it amongst ourselves. We felt that imperative to win.

When we were exhausted, we'd remind ourselves how much our outcome mattered. If we flopped, if the money that the NBA and USA Basketball put up to keep us together for a year didn't show on the court, we feared the promise of stateside professional women's basketball would die on the vine. Our team carried that burden for the whole time that we were together, all the way up until and through the Olympic finals.

Tara did what she needed to do. If she had to do it all over again, would she do it the same way? Knowing Tara, I'd say she probably would. But if I had to do it over, and this is me speaking as a woman over fifty, I would change my part in the dynamic. I would've talked to Tara a little bit more. I would've spoken up even more on behalf of the team. Of course, I was only twenty-six years old. Trying to make my first Olympic team. There was no way I was not going to fall in line. That's what we all did. Because we were willing to do anything to represent our country and put women's basketball on the map.

That said, I did get away with comments no other player would dare make. For example, I called Tara out when I thought she was favoring the opposing team during scrimmages. Me, I got a little spice to what I'm doing. I think in some regards, Tara respected that. She gave me leeway. She'd coached me on the B team before I got cut in 1992. Seen me play at Virginia, when she coached Stanford. I suspect she figured she could deal with one of me in the mix. But she couldn't have taken five.

I remember when we first began officially training as a team together, I was in the best shape of my life. If the Olympics had started then, I would have been the starting point guard. It wasn't even close. Then my knee began swelling every practice like a water balloon. I needed a quick surgery. Got one. Then I broke my hand.

While I was out rehabbing, Teresa Edwards forged ahead. She was playing incredibly well, running our team, even though she wasn't a point guard. Tara built her into a point guard.

When I returned, I wanted my old spot, but even I could see Teresa was crushing it. By the time I fully healed, I was behind, nowhere near where I began. No matter how hard I tried, I couldn't get back in my best form. I lost my starting spot, had to settle for coming off the bench. I was deflated.

Instead of shutting down, I made the decision to lean in and do everything in my power to get the second team ready to rock and roll. Growth!

Leading the best players in the world was an awesome responsibility, and not one I took lightly. I knew my teammates were looking to me to meet every challenge. It didn't matter how tired I was, I rose to the occasion. Letting them down would be letting our country down, letting women's basketball down, and there was no way I'd allow that to happen.

When I took ownership of the second team, I did it with flair. If you watch clip reels from back in the day, you'll see that my flavor stands out. There weren't that many women playing that way then. I know Tara would've preferred that I didn't play that way. But I'm going to tell you this. When I came off the bench, I was going to make some magic happen. I was going to make some heads spin.

Some people like my style, some people don't, but at the end of the day at least they know where I'm coming from and that's a good place to be. I made it my personal mission to make sure our morale was high and we were ready for anything.

I would throw an assist over my shoulder. I would throw bounce passes between my legs. I was strategic. I made sure that Rebecca shined, too, because again, she had the hardest time. I was like, okay, here you go. Be here. Take this. Boom. And she would deliver.

All these many years later, people remember me from those passes. They don't remember I only started one game.

While we were in Atlanta, we never stayed in the Olympic Village. There was mandated gender equity in USA Basketball, so legally they had to treat us the same way they treated the men's Dream Team. The male players stayed in hotels. Nice hotels. Which meant we got to also. Even our per diem was on par with the men's. When we saw the amount, we couldn't believe it. It was damn near half of our paycheck.

I always say, playing for your country is like no other experience in sports. It doesn't matter where you're from or what personal achievements you had prior to putting on the red, white, and blue. Once you're in uniform, you feel the unity of our country. You feel it like no other. You get pulled into that energy and you discover what representing your country is all about. You instantaneously become patriotic on a different level. You feel more American.

A lot of people don't like American players for one reason or another, but make no mistake, we work hard. Everything that we've won, we've earned.

As a coach, you fight. You fight for what you think is right, and Tara was no different. Everybody who's charged with something as pressure-packed as the Olympics should do it their way because when it's all said and done, you're going to be the one left holding the bag or holding the gold medal.

What Tara did in the run-up to Atlanta, for all the controversy, worked. By the time the Games commenced, our nerves were nonexistent. It felt like: Bam! It's showtime! We started playing and realized no one could touch us. I think our lowest margin of victory was eighteen points.

On August 4, 1996, we defeated Brazil 111–87 in the gold medal game in front of 32,997 fans.

Thinking about her now, with the softening passage of time, I feel nothing but respect for Tara. She's a genius. A savant. I probably went through my biggest learning spurt under her. Tara, she broke basketball down. (She broke us down, too!) My style's not necessarily the same as hers, but I understand the responsibility she faced and relate to her passion for the game.

I've even ended up borrowing some of Tara's technique and implemented it in my coaching. Early in my career, I took her exact Olympic summer workout, the twelve-week program that tormented so many of us players. I told my players to postmark their exercise logs by a certain date. I even revived the loathed Breakfast Club. My thinking was, if these young women do half of this, we're going to be in pretty darn good shape.

The November prior to the Atlanta Olympics, Tara took us to the Georgia Dome. We were on our way to play an exhibition game in Athens. The dome was set up for a football game, but Tara marched us all to the middle of the field anyway. Then she asked Teresa Edwards to bring out the gold medal she'd won in 1988.

Tara stood us in a line and draped the medal around each of our necks, one by one. She wanted us to feel the weight and possibility of the future.

And what a future it was. Not only did we emerge from that long year as the best in the world, but the professional women's leagues were born as a result.

The momentum we'd built over the twelve months leading to the Olympics had paid off. We'd put our talent on display and revealed our draw to fans who were eager to see women play ball. Behind the scenes various stakeholders were ready to make the leap to supporting stateside women's leagues.

I remember like it was yesterday when the ABL founders came to me and asked me to be a part of the launch of the league. They offered $150,000 a year to be a founding member. Everybody on our national team said they were going to play for the ABL. When the WNBA was announced a few months later, Lisa, Sheryl, and Rebecca decided they were going to join that league instead.

At the time, we felt the more, the merrier! More job opportunities. More growth. We were all for it.

I played two years in the ABL before my knees decided they'd had enough. By then I'd had eight arthroscopic surgeries. The ABL ran a traditional basketball season over eight months. The WNBA season was just five. I couldn't keep logging that many games and stay healthy. My body needed a break, or I wasn't going to last.

I hung up my sneakers with the ABL and joined the WNBA so I could play fewer months but for more years. It ended up being the right decision, because the following season the ABL went under. I'd made the jump just in time.

In 1999, I was the ninth overall pick for the Charlotte Sting. Not long after, our team was headed to the WNBA finals, where I was able to compete against my former teammate Lisa Leslie. Sharing that spotlight with her was beyond cool. I ended up being on the losing end of the stick, she even shed a tear over it, but it was still worth it to celebrate that epic moment together.

I'm grateful I got a chance to experience both leagues. When I was growing up, most women were forced to retire from basketball after college. Now the WNBA is a carrot dangled in front of every young woman who aspires to keep playing. A rising athlete might play a bit harder, she might give more, dedicate herself more, because she knows there's light at the end of the tunnel. Women players today don't know life without the WNBA. And that's a glorious thing. For all of women's sports.

In 2005 I was traded to the Houston Comets. I announced

to the press that that season would be my last. People assumed it was the knees talking. But in truth, it was my heart. Every player develops a strong threshold for pain. I was used to hurting. But the nagging feeling in my chest was something I couldn't push through or get over. My instincts were stirring me to move on.

When it comes down to it, I played in the WNBA a year longer than I should have. I forced myself to stay in the league because I wanted to be absolutely sure I was done. I needed to get playing out of my system so I wouldn't look back with regret. And I haven't.

My body was done. And the psychological effort of gutting through what it took to get me court-ready proved to be too much. I didn't want to train anymore. I wanted to train others. To mentor. To coach. I've never looked back.

Which in some ways is astonishing. I never thought I'd voluntarily stop playing. You had to fight to keep me off the court. But then I grew older, and I realized I'd done everything I could hope to as a player. There would have been something sad about keeping on. Like the guest who stays at the party too long, after everyone else has gone home.

I'd left it all on the court. Done what I had to do. Gotten what I wanted. Now it was time to do that for others.

In my office, I have my Olympic jerseys framed and lined up. For the most part I ignore them. They're just part of my everyday.

On the odd days when they do catch my eye, they take me back. I travel in my mind to that place and time. The 1996 jersey is special, because it's my first, the goal that kept me driven and determined during those dark months abroad. To win a gold medal at the age of twenty-six was pretty darn gratifying. Surreal even.

The 2004 jersey prompts a different flavor of memory. The gold medal game versus Australia in Athens was my last dance. I picked up a foul at the start of the game. Sixty seconds later, another one. Two too many. Off the court I went. I always joke that that game was when I learned how to be an assistant coach, because I was seated next to them for so long.

When I returned to the game in the fourth quarter, I went in saying to my team as I went, "We only win gold." With five minutes left and Australia leading, I made two of the biggest baskets of my career, essentially sealing the victory for Team USA.

I firmly believe if I didn't have that initial disappointment of not making the '92 team, I wouldn't have appreciated my first Olympic gold nearly as much. If I'd opted for the easy route, quit my team in Spain, not cleared that developmental hurdle, I would not have become a three-time Olympian, three-time gold medalist, two-time assistant coach, or head coach of an Olympic team.

Sometimes life throws you a curveball. And then you have to do what you don't want to do to get what you want. When I tell my players that, I hope they know I was once exactly where they are. A lonely kid on her own, fighting to be seen, striving to see the possibilities that lie within, watching Kid 'n Play in her room.

No One Does It Alone

Over the past few years, I've become friendly with Judge Clifton Newman, a huge Gamecocks fan. He's the same judge who presided over the Alexander Murdaugh trial for the murder of his wife and son. In 2021, while I was coaching in Japan during the Olympics, my eyes were glued to the Court TV coverage of another trial of his, involving a University of South Carolina student who had been murdered. When I returned stateside and he learned of my true-crime obsession, Judge Newman invited me to attend his next trial, a local double murder.

"If you feel like it," he said. Which I most certainly did.

I was in that courtroom every day. I did worry I was a distraction. People recognized who I was. They probably wondered,

Why is she in here? I stressed about where I was seated. Does it look like I am here supporting the defendant? Is it like a wedding? Am I on the wrong side?

I stuck it out through the whole week. When both sides rested their case, I walked up to the prosecutor and their team and asked whether I could see what they were showing the jury. I wanted to eyeball the crime photos. Even though I had an appointment that afternoon, I couldn't bring myself to leave the scene. I wanted to see the entire proceeding through.

I acknowledge this is an odd way to spend my precious free time. I wasn't into true crime stuff as a child. I think I became interested because in my life now, it's an escape. I've watched *Dateline* for more than twenty years. Whenever I can, I pull up Court TV on my iPad and soak up every twist and turn. I get a rise out of it. It feeds something in my morbidly curious soul. It's also, oddly enough, a lesson in teamwork.

Hear me out. A high-stakes trial involves two teams playing against each other. There is strategy, there is rehearsal (or practice), there is the hard labor of fact-finding and research (Xs and Os), there is meticulous preparation (no lawyer worth his or her salt ever asks a question of a witness that they don't already know the answer to), and there is intricate choreography, knowing which team member performs best under what conditions. No one wins a case alone. Showboaters may carry the day in legal dramas, but in a real-world trial, every member of your team has a critical role in the outcome, even those folks you never see behind the scenes. See, just like basketball!

I guess what I'm saying is I love teamwork in all its forms. Watching any group come together to work toward a specific goal with excellence and competence is mesmerizing to me. Learning how people react to certain instances, good or bad. Problem-solving. In the trenches of competition, you gain intimate friendships. Some teams overcome. Others flail and crash. Why?

That's the heart of it for me. The *why*. What makes some folks succeed while others never do? You can put together a team on paper that looks as if it should dominate, but the players never gel. You can have an assortment of underdogs who rise up and achieve what seems impossible. And, depending on how many players you have on your team, you inevitably find multiple answers to those whys.

Bringing a team, any type of team, to success involves a million moving parts and constant microcalculations. The math is complex. But it's never boring. And it's not something a person achieves on their own.

I know all this now, but before I started coaching, I could never have fathomed how stimulating and rewarding it is to puzzle together a playing team, with the help of a coaching team. Coaching was on my radar as much as competing in the Miss America pageant. Then, in April of 2000, I received a call from Temple University. They asked whether I'd ever considered becoming a coach.

"Not a day in my life," I responded. I was a player. I couldn't imagine myself yelling at people from the sidelines. I couldn't picture myself off the court, without the ball in my hand.

A couple of days later they rang again and asked whether I would be open to meeting Dave O'Brien, then Temple's athletic director. I was already in Philadelphia with the US Olympic team. We had a scrimmage scheduled (which they knew). It's my hometown (which they also knew). There was no wiggle room. I felt I should show the AD respect. Out of courtesy I agreed to meet.

I told myself I'd walk over there and let him down easy. My intention was to meet O'Brien, who I expected would ask me about coming to coach, after which I would respectfully thank him for his consideration, then formally decline. I didn't even dress the part. I wore jeans and a T-shirt. Let's just say, the appointment didn't go exactly as I had planned.

From the jump O'Brien completely ignored my passive resistance. He circumvented my arguments about lack of interest, instead challenging me on my abilities. He asked me directly, "Are you a leader?"

Was I a leader?

I was flabbergasted. I'm a point guard. I'm basically the captain on every team that I've played on. My whole history in that position is leading the team.

I looked O'Brien directly in the eye and answered, "Yes, of course, I can lead."

To his credit, that's when he knew he had me. I'd swallowed the bait.

Then he followed up with, "Do you think you could meet the challenge of turning around this women's basketball program?"

That one I didn't answer. But I always give O'Brien credit for approaching me with the precise thing that drives me. He lured me into coaching in the cleverest way, by planting the seed of an obstacle to overcome.

After our chat, O'Brien wondered whether I might be able to quickly say hi to a few of his colleagues. Sure, I said. Then he led me into a room with what looked to be a formal committee of about a dozen people. I found myself unwittingly walking into a job interview. It was unorthodox, but I admired the AD's nerve.

They sat me at the head of the table and started firing questions like a tennis ball launcher. Ping, ping, ping. What do you want to do next in the sport? What do you see yourself doing in five years?

"Playing in the WNBA," I said.

I was honest and frank. I didn't hold anything back because, as I kept telling myself, *I didn't want the job.*

I can't recall what else I said or how long the impromptu interrogation lasted. But it hardly mattered. My qualifications were well-known throughout Philly. And for my part, as soon as the AD offered me the job as a dare of sorts, to turn the Temple women's basketball program into a point of pride for my hometown, I was in, hook, line, and sinker. I was constitutionally incapable of walking away from a challenge. I wanted to prove I could do it.

Barely two weeks after that meeting, I was named the incoming head coach of the women's basketball team at Temple University. A position I would hold a few short blocks from where I grew up.

I was twenty-nine and had absolutely no idea what I had walked into.

I had zero coaching or program-building experience. And the demands on my time were already too many. I was an active member of the WNBA's Charlotte Sting and the point guard for the 2000 US national team that was gearing up for the Sydney Olympic Games. I hadn't just accepted a job I'd never done before; I took on that job on top of several other arduous responsibilities.

I remember freaking out, thinking, I can't be responsible for young people! They're practically my age! I'm younger than their parents! The very idea of being some sort of authority figure stand-in was overwhelming.

What buoyed me was that I knew basketball, and basketball had yet to let me down. I jumped into coaching the way I attacked every other test I'd faced in the past. I dove headfirst into the pool. I had a template in Jen Rizzotti, who in 1999 was hired to coach at Hartford while still playing for the WNBA's Houston, and then Cleveland, team. When I wondered how I'd make time to sleep, eat, train, what my day planner would even look like—I would look to Jen and think, *Well, she made it work.*

The first thing I did was hire Coach Shawn Campbell from UVA as my first assistant. I knew he had program knowledge and would help me organize. Then I filled out the staff with other assistant coaches who had teaching experience and could relate to the players. I was Kermit the Frog green. I needed a seasoned support team that would provide me instant credibility, as well as be a critical source of lived-in, battle-tested knowledge.

After acclimating myself to a rundown of all the components that make up a college basketball program, I set about delegating responsibilities. Initially I wasn't comfortable giving up control, but necessity prevailed. Between training, playing, and coaching, I was stretched thin as parchment paper. There were not enough hours in the day to dedicate to internalizing all the intricacies of a Division I basketball program.

Outsourcing the work proved essential to our success. Each coach had an area of expertise and took ownership of their part. I was able to oversee their work and learn on the fly at the same time, trusting that the team we assembled would keep the trains running. And they did. We posted a winning record our first season.

What I settled on for my approach as a coach was to treat it like a huddle—something, as a point guard, I was familiar with. A point guard is the conductor on the floor. An extension of the head coach on the sideline. I wholeheartedly believe that coming in as a point guard was the primary reason I was able to transition into the job. If I'd been a center, who knows?

Once we started playing games, I encountered other learning curves. There are long media time-outs, two and a half minutes. We'd be gathered around the bench, I'd fill the team in on what I saw, what we needed to do. I'd give my take and by thirty seconds, I would have said all I needed to. And we'd just be sitting there, the players blinking at me, like, *You know you've got two more minutes.*

Obviously, I adjusted. I learned how to say more, give more, do more, be more. Learning to coach from the ground up was all-consuming. Especially on top of my continuing to play professional basketball. I made five WNBA All-Star teams and won an Olympic gold medal in my first six years coaching the Temple Owls. That's some next-level unlocked multitasking.

In some ways my simultaneous jobs were an asset. Instead of having me go out and recruit, we'd dangle, "Come see our coach kill it in the WNBA!" Because ultimately that's what these young women wanted for themselves. It was a powerful incentive. And it worked. I could get in any door.

That didn't mean I was going to land the commitment from a recruit. But my time in the WNBA, as well as the Olympics, along with the accolades I'd racked up, did grease the wheels. Any player signing on at Temple could trust that I knew exactly what it took to succeed at the highest levels, because I was literally there doing it in real time.

I also turned to the community of North Philly for support and, unsurprisingly, they showed up. Our arena was packed and boisterous. We got great press coverage. Temple wins felt like wins for our neighborhood. In a move that rocked my world, my father began attending games. He tucked himself away in the rafters so as not to be noticed.

My dad had never wanted me to play basketball. He was old-school about gender roles. Moreover, he thought trying to make a career out of basketball was a waste of time. It was the eighties. He had no perspective as to where the game could or would take me. He couldn't imagine women's sports ever being a thing, let alone a way to earn a living. To give him the benefit of the doubt, he probably thought discouraging my playing was in my best interest.

Now here he was cheering on not only me but an entire women's team. After my dad passed away on December 1, 2006, I was told he'd kept a box of my press clippings. That he'd pull that box out and show the saved articles to anyone who came by to visit. He was proud of me, of what basketball provided. In the end he finally understood.

Within a fairly short time, Temple became a March Madness fixture, but it took work to get there. The smartest early decision I made was begging veteran coach Lisa Boyer to join our staff. I called her every day. No, seriously, every day. I got to where I didn't even say hello. I'd call. She'd answer. And I'd bark, "Say you're coming." She'd pass. Unequivocally. "Hell no!" This went on for two years. Ultimately, I wore her down.

Boyer relented in 2002. She'd head-coached the ABL's Philadelphia Rage before moving on to the WNBA's Cleveland Rockers from 1998 to 2002. During her time with the Rockers, she became the first woman (thirteen years before Becky Hammon) to hold an NBA coaching job as an assistant for the Cleveland Cavaliers.

Whom you hire to be in the foxhole with you is vital. Boyer knew me as a player from the ABL and was positive I had the basketball IQ and leadership skills to thrive. She rightly surmised that what I needed from her was organization, player-specific advice, and to keep the larger Temple program engine humming while I was away trying to win gold medals and WNBA championships.

An expert in all the ins and outs of every angle of coaching, Boyer came on board with tireless resolve and showed me what it took to be a great all-around coach. Even so, there were many nights when I thought, *I really should have gone into broadcasting*. I'm a master compartmentalizer, but I was utterly exhausted, paddling like mad to keep my head above water. Although we were winning and building a solid foundation for

Temple, I found myself doubting I'd made the right choice to take on coaching.

Then came our first A-10 Championship in 2002.

It was the end of the game against St. Joe's at the Liacouras. There were two minutes left, and we were down by two points. The objective was to get the ball in the corner, but my point guard kept missing the play. I'm screaming, but she can't see or hear me. I call a time-out and draw up the play again, boring my eyes into hers as I say, "Reverse the freaking ball!" She looks at me deadpan and says, "Yeah, okay, Coach."

We put our hands in, chant "Win," then the team takes the floor. I call the exact same play and lo and behold, my point guard reverses the ball. She gets it to Natalia Isaac, who drains a three in the corner. St. Joe's bolts down court but can't convert. We rebound, our player gets fouled and sinks a pair of free throws. The balance is tipped. Time runs out. That's all she wrote. We'd captured the school's first Atlantic 10 Conference tournament title.

When we won that game, that was the moment I stopped doubting forever whether I'd made the right choice to become a coach. It wasn't that it was so spectacular a game. More that we'd locked in.

All of us—every player, coach, assistant, staff member— had come together and competed as a unit. I didn't know before that night how gratifying that could feel. The puzzle pieces snapping into place. Winning takes more than five players. It takes more than a great coach. It takes the whole synchronized orchestra making music together. No one does it alone.

I coached for six years while playing in the WNBA. Then

stayed on at Temple two years after I retired. While I was there, the Owls went to six NCAA tournaments and earned the east division championship multiple times. In 2005, we finished the regular season 16–0, becoming the first team in A-10 history to go undefeated. All those achievements felt great. I loved the young ladies we recruited. They were tough, fearless. They believed in themselves. They wanted to win as much as I did . . .

Which was why leaving my job at Temple was like ripping out a piece of my heart.

The reality was, after eight years, I knew I had gone as far as I could in Philly. We'd gotten to the point where we were getting out-talented. During the NCAA tournament, we could never get past the first or second round. Eight years in, we'd been to the tournament six times and hit that wall every time.

Being the competitor that I am, I wanted to win a national championship, and it was becoming evident, to me at least, that I couldn't get that done at Temple.

At the end of the day, it's North Philly, and with multiple choices about where to send your kid, many parents opt for a more traditional campus environment. Fact is, universities located in cities can struggle with recruiting. They often lack the bells and whistles available on larger campuses with bigger budgets and more sprawling grounds. Perks such as modern facilities or team transportation via charter plane versus by bus, for example. A Candace Parker was not going to come to Temple over a Tennessee, you know? That was not something I could change. I wasn't actively shopping myself, but it was becoming clear that to have a shot at my goal of an NCAA title, I was going to need to coach elsewhere.

Alabama came after me first in 2005. I visited the campus. I liked the athletic director. But I couldn't see myself living in Alabama.

A year or two later, the South Carolina position came open, and I got calls feeling out my interest, which was, as I told them, piqued. The SEC, as a whole, has more budget, more big-league swagger. South Carolina was located on an old-fashioned, telegenic campus, which made attracting re-cruits much smoother. And it was in a geographic area with a good amount of regional basketball talent. I liked my chances.

I was drawn to the fact that USC was part of the SEC and its storied legacy in women's basketball. Pat Summitt was in this league, Andy Landers, Melanie Balcomb, all these legend-ary coaches. I was looking to refine my skills, rise to compete with the best. The cherry on top was that my parents were orig-inally from South Carolina. I needed to have some connection to the place I was going to live, likely for many years. My mom was getting older. If I took the job coaching the Gamecocks, she could reunite with her siblings. She could come home.

I went down for a visit, stayed overnight at a hotel. The next day a Realtor escorted me around the city. Columbia was bigger than I expected. When I'd visited the state as a child, it was all dirt roads and double-wides. When it was time for lunch, I think they got all the Black people they could find to come sit down with me. They even called in a Black community leader. It was funny but nice that they made the effort.

I soaked in every second. I was trying to feel myself in the space. In my head, questioning, *Can I do it? It's the South.* I was born and raised in a city. I knew I could survive anywhere because I made my way through college and international ball, but I wanted to make sure that personally, professionally, a southern town was a fit for me. No one was going to talk me into it. It had to hit me organically.

My main interview was with the AD Eric Hyman, who was fifty-seven at the time. A few members of the staff came to Philly and picked me up in the school plane. I can remember his right hand, Marcy Girton, telling me something like, listen to Eric, don't talk a whole lot. That's how I took it anyway. No need to ask me twice. Tell me not to talk a whole lot and I'm good to go. Preaching to the choir.

My attitude going into the meeting was, I have a job. I'm comfortable in my job. They are the ones who need a coach. When I got to the interview, I wasn't nervous. But I was subdued.

They began by asking me questions about connecting with donors, going to fund-raising events. That was a bit of a red flag for me. My interview at Temple had been much different. Then again, Temple probably didn't need to do as much due diligence as South Carolina, because they knew me. South Carolina saw I'd had success at Temple. With a 172–80 overall record, I was the winningest coach in its women's basketball history and the fastest to reach a hundred victories. USC was confident I could coach. What they didn't know was whether I was prepared to leave the city I loved for them. Whether I could network in that atmosphere. They asked a few questions about how I build relationships with young people. And then, somewhat abruptly, it was over.

Overall, the energy in the room was muted. Sparks did not

fly. When I left to go home, I was certain that they didn't want to hire me.

Turns out, my assumption was correct. After meeting me, South Carolina remained firmly on the fence. A day later, my phone rang.

"Eric wants to come back up to Philly to talk. He didn't really get a feel for you." I understood why.

Soon enough, Eric came to visit. We went to a nearby Starbucks for coffee. As we were making our way down the street, people shouted out, "Hey, Dawn! What's up?" Some yelled, "Dawn, don't leave us!" The press had leaked that South Carolina was sniffing around. They didn't know Eric was the AD.

For the whole duration of the walk, folks were calling my name, waving, smiling, snapping pictures, fist bumping. Eric witnessed all of that. He saw what I meant to Philly and Philly to me. How I'd made an impact. It couldn't have been more obvious that I cared about my community, and my community had my back.

An hour later, he left for South Carolina knowing I was his coach.

In the background at USC, I knew they were considering the University of Tennessee's Holly Warlick. She was an exceptional networker. Eric was weighing the pros and cons of a talented coach who could have a beer with the boosters against the likes of me, who was maybe a bit awkward but was all about the endgame of a national championship title. After our Philly visit, Eric told his team back in South Carolina, "I can handle the boosters. Dawn is going to handle getting us a win."

I felt ready. To move on, to be charged with building a

national championship team. Philly would always be my number one, but to grow in the sport I had to leave. Columbia was the perfect spot to bring my mom. She never would have considered anywhere else in the country. She would've just stayed rooted in Philly. She'd had a small stroke, and I wanted her close so I could take care of her. The stars were all aligning to bring us to South Carolina together.

At Temple I figured out how to build a roster, how to inspire players, how to convince parents to trust me with their children's futures. As vitally, my time there taught me there is no weakness in not being able to do everything yourself. I absorbed as much as I could, then I deputized. Good leaders know there's only upside when you allow yourself to learn from others. Hire the best and empower them to do their part. It's a habit I've carried through all the phases and corners of my life.

I packed those and many other lessons with me when I left for Columbia. (I packed up Coach Boyer, too.) Just as at Temple, the team I have around me at USC makes sure I stay on track. Everywhere you look, I've got people who complement where I'm weak, who supplement my deficiencies. Some leaders like to pretend they don't have shortcomings and they're good at everything. That every success stems from them. To that I say—oh, hell no.

It's smarter and more efficient to do the things you do best and allow others to do the same. I surround myself with talented, down-to-earth people who are focused on being successful but who also know what it takes. You need to be confident that you won't allow each other to falter.

I continue to see myself as a point guard. Managing, facilitating, doing what I need to do to set people up to win. On the staffs I put together, there are no princesses. If you put on airs, you don't last long. I always say, if there's water spilled on the court, I'll grab a mop. There's no job too big or too small for any one of us to do. It's key to assemble a team that allows you to be authentic, so no energy is wasted with pretense. You want colleagues who both lift you up and aren't afraid to deliver harsh reality checks when necessary. It's a balancing act.

As Anita Baker sang, "I hope you see that you can lean on me / And together we can calm a stormy sea."

Trust what Anita is saying. No one does it alone.

Sometimes I still can't believe I'm a coach. You gotta be a little nuts to make coaching a career choice. I'm basically resting my livelihood on the decisions of teenagers. Think back to the decisions you made as a teenager. Crazy, right?

If I'm being honest, I've kept coaching to test myself. I'm fueled by challenges. I have an insatiable desire for the process. For unearthing the why.

After I graduated college, I never thought I would be put in a position again to win a national championship. But coaching found me. And national titles followed.

I cherished my first championship win as a coach as much as I ever could have as a player. I'd already won medals and titles. Make no mistake, I love winning. Those honors mean the world to me. And yet, the depth of emotion I felt when South Carolina clinched our championship win against Mississippi State in 2017 was like nothing I'd ever known.

We'd played the Bulldogs twice already in the season. I knew their strengths and weaknesses. The strategy was to own the real estate under the basket, dominate in the paint. The plan unfolded seamlessly.

With a 67–55 victory over Mississippi State, I became the second Black coach to win the NCAA championship since Carolyn Peck coached Purdue to victory in 1999. As the last seconds ticked off, I hugged my assistant coaches. Confetti fell like rain.

Forward A'ja Wilson was named the Final Four's most outstanding player, scoring twenty-three points in the final. I'd told her when I asked her to play for South Carolina that if she committed to us, we were going to win a national championship. That night she told the media she took me at my word, "and here we are."

As the victory celebration continued, I cut down the net, draped it around my neck. I paraded around the court with the trophy. Joined in as my players danced and cried and embraced each other.

When you see the impact of a winning season on the faces of the players who trusted and worked tirelessly for you all year, to know they will have doors flung open wide, and better and bigger opportunities in their futures because of the culmination of that shared effort—there's simply nothing more powerful for a coach.

I always say I got into coaching to advance the game of basketball. I've stayed to advance the lives of young people.

After the Gamecocks won in 2017, I gave a miniature version of the national championship trophy to every one of my former players from Temple and South Carolina. I gave one to every coach I ever worked alongside. I got trophies for my Virginia teammates, too. Basically, I gave a replica to every single person I could think of who had a hand in making that win happen.

I had teammates and former players and coaching staff who believed in that vision. Maybe we didn't get it done on the timeline we wanted. But all of them were essential pieces of the team that landed me where I was in 2017.

To me, all those people were as much a part of earning that title as I was. Because really, it's the individuals who trusted in you before you were able to pull off a win who are the most important people in your trajectory. The realization of this dream carried far beyond me.

I was built by those people and those experiences, grateful for all who had inched me along my journey, and I felt they should be acknowledged. Winning is always a culmination of all that came before. It's always a product of team. No one does it alone.

Each trophy had a small plate with the etched words "Because of you."

People over Process

The University of South Carolina offered me the head coaching job on my birthday, May 4, 2008. I couldn't wait to get started. I was charged with turning the women's basketball program around. Personally, I wanted to bring national prominence to the school. I was done losing in the first or second round of the NCAA tournament.

I had a $500,000 buyout after exiting my contract with Temple. USC had to pay that on top of my $650,000 salary. After being here for a while, I figured out not everybody was thrilled the university had paid me that much money. There were whispers that it was an issue for the board. The AD had to fight on my behalf. As a former women's basketball coach, our then AD was invested in our success in a way others were not. He also had a prescient vision of where the women's game was heading.

After I formally began at USC, I kept hearing about how the baseball coach, Ray Tanner (now the current AD), earned less than I did. The pay disparity would come up in conversations and in the press. My general response was along the lines of, "Oh, really?" Baseball is a big thing in South Carolina. When I was directly asked by different media outlets about why I should be paid more than the baseball coach, for a long time I didn't answer. I kept it moving. But the question didn't go away. The media kept raising the fact that I was outearning a male coach. Finally, I clapped back, explaining, "I made more than the baseball coach before I got here. You think I'm going to come here and take a pay cut?"

That put a stop to that line of inquiry, but the uneasy dynamics stayed in place. The social and political climate was different from that in Philly. It felt a bit like being back in Virginia, where I needed to suss out and adjust to a distinct mode of communication. While I enjoyed being in South Carolina and was excited about the future we could build there, my first few years on the job were tricky. In fact, there were times when I thought my coaching at a school that was in the toughest conference in the country and consistently fell in last place was professional suicide.

I had to build the program from the bottom up. Not knowing anyone. It felt like heading overseas all over again. I was a stranger in a strange land.

I never felt more so than during our first season, when we got our heads beat in. We were 8–21. The second year was slightly better, but still not good. I wasn't used to losing. And I certainly wasn't patient. It wasn't until 2012, four years into my tenure, that we made it to the NCAA tournament for the first time. Those four years tested me in ways I did not see coming.

I knew there would be building seasons. In theory, I accepted that fact. In reality, it tried my will. When I took the job, I built my staff with trusted allies from Temple and elsewhere. I brought in Coach Lisa Boyer to be my first assistant. Boyer was my right hand.

Let me take a beat to tell you a bit more about the type of woman Lisa Boyer is. Boyer has been my North Star since I was twenty-eight years old, starting in 1996, when she coached the ABL's Philadelphia Rage and I joined the team as point guard. We've been ride-or-die ever since.

I can talk to Boyer about anything. Basketball, life, fashion, family, grief, pop culture. If I want a straight answer, she's going to give me one. Over the years, she's sacrificed in countless ways to help me build my career. I've rarely seen anyone as devoted to women's basketball, myself included.

When I was the women's national team head coach, Boyer served as a scout and court coach for USA Basketball. She was with our team at the 2020 Tokyo Olympics, where the United States brought home its seventh straight gold medal. At Temple she had my back as we made five NCAA tournaments and three Atlantic 10 tournament titles in six seasons. As South Carolina's associate head coach, she's been indispensable.

Throughout these decades together, I would not have been nearly as successful without her expertise, her tirelessness, and—to be honest—her obsessiveness. I mean, she ruminates on *every single thing*. When I want to not think about basketball, I can trust she is thinking about basketball.

Our players describe us as an old married couple. We bicker. We tease each other. We fight. Whatever the mood of the day, we let each other be exactly who we are. There's more than a bit of yin and yang in our styles. She's chatty, a talker. I'm not. She's anxious, I'm mostly chill. She's earnest. I'm a bit of a joker.

When I played for her in the ABL, I'd tease her that she was taking years off my life. Now I've had my revenge, taking years off hers, since we've coached together for so long.

Boyer has watched and helped me grow from a newbie coach to a place of prominence. Every single step. Like I do, she sees our players as her children. Like I do, she wants them to succeed and lead beyond USC, to have all the chances and opportunities they yearn for.

That level of compatibility and comfort is rare in any relationship, let alone a professional one. I call Boyer my warrior. If we're going into battle, she's the one I want by my side. Which is why I brought her into the Gamecocks fold on day one.

After Boyer, I hired Olympic teammates Nikki McCray and Carla McGhee to be my second and third assistants, respectively. The bonds we'd forged during our time on Team USA stayed tight, and I knew I could count on them to keep pushing as we'd done all those years ago.

Nikki had SEC experience as a player. She'd started coaching two years before I took the South Carolina job. Once I decided I was headed south, I cornered her on the road: "You're coming, right?" Nikki was like, "Yeah, I'm down." She was nervous about leaving her job and wanted to give a month's notice. "We don't have a month!" I shot back.

I had the same conversation with Carla, who was coaching at Auburn. I wasn't accepting no for an answer. Soon enough, I'd assembled my dream team.

The first thing we did as a group was visit all the players on the current Gamecocks roster. We discovered that the best players were MIA. It turned out that some members of the exiting women's basketball staff had advised them to join teams elsewhere. When it came to exceptional talent, we had, well, none.

The players who remained were eager to have us. That was the good news. The bad news was that their goals didn't align with ours. When it came to basketball, many of the players we inherited viewed the team as a hobby. They got accepted into the university on a basketball scholarship, but their true passion was elsewhere. They didn't want to be pros. They didn't eat, sleep, and breathe the game. They were using the scholarship as a means to an end. We simply weren't cut from the same cloth, and because of that, our levels never matched.

Practically, that meant as soon as I began coaching them to win championships, they boarded the struggle bus. As did I.

Now, you must understand, when I worked at Temple, we hit the ground running. All our players wanted to win. They wanted to play hard. They wanted to play for me.

At South Carolina I assumed it would be the same. That we'd come in with roaring passion, change their mindset from that of the conference doormats to a competitive and viable conference threat. That our players would be hungry out of the gate, eager to go, go, GO!

Instead, I was met with . . . no, no, nope. A whole lot of nope.

I implemented every strategy I'd used to spur performance at Temple to no avail. I'd press the players, "Don't you want to win?" They said they did, kind of. As long as it didn't take too much time and effort. Basketball was low on their list of priorities. And really, why would they invest time and energy if they had no intention of playing once school ended? That mentality wasn't wrong, necessarily, but it was a brick wall when it came to growing the program. I began to consider that I might have made a mistake moving to USC.

It didn't help that many of the people I consulted when making my decision about South Carolina had encouraged me not to take the job. Most of them warned that there was no way I could turn the program around, and when I failed, it would tank my nascent coaching career. In my dark nights of the soul, I began to believe them. I found myself consumed with self-doubt.

My coaching staff and I often deliberated during those first few years, fretting about what we'd gotten ourselves into. On the bench, Boyer sat to my left, Nikki to my right, and Carla was next to Boyer. When things were going pear-shaped on the court, I'd glance down the bench and Nikki, blocking my view with her body, turning sideways, would say, "Uh-uh, don't do it. Ain't nothing down there for you." And we'd have to laugh because she was right. When it came to talent and enthusiasm, the cupboard was bare.

It was hard. I wanted the team to evolve faster, to rack up those Ws. I was trying to force aspiration out of them. Every practice was a rallying-the-troops day. I got frustrated because the players couldn't do what I needed them to do. They weren't equipped. I may as well have been asking them to speak Portuguese underwater. For the first time in my coaching career, I felt helpless. I couldn't break the inertia.

I obsessed over what I had done to make it work at Temple. The kids there weren't offended by my colorful language. They weren't scared off by my death stares or by my roll of the eyes when they made a mistake. They got me.

While I was coaching in Philly, the team would sit and watch my daily WNBA workouts after our practices. They saw me at the 2000 and 2004 Olympics. They would drive down to Charlotte to watch my pro games in the summer. Maybe my being the living example of what I expected from them made the difference. Problem was that by the time I started coaching at USC, my playing days were long over.

I wasn't tuned in to it in the moment, but in a way, some of the fault lay with me. I was putting process before people. I expected my prior coaching practices to apply to a whole new group without adjusting my approach. South Carolina was not Temple. I was square-peg, round-holing.

In my defense, I'd never run into young people who didn't want to be professional athletes. Back in the projects, those kids all wanted to be pros. They may not have had the talent, but they had the mindset. None of that ethos applied at USC. I had to find a new way to lead.

My second year at South Carolina, we were able to bring on a couple of good players who inched the needle forward, but most of our team still consisted of people who didn't love basketball. Quick coaching fact: Your team is going to reflect the attitude of most of your players. If most of your team worships basketball, you've got a shot. If most of your team is marking time, you're never going to get past the starting block.

And so it went for several seasons. Try as we might, we didn't field enough players who had the passion to pull us over the hump. Staying motivated in the face of an extended dance remix of defeat was demoralizing.

Thankfully, while I was figuring out how to make it work in South Carolina, Eric the AD kept any internal pressure from the school off my radar. He'd warned when he hired me that building the women's program was going to take three years minimum. To which I said, "What are you talking about?" Three years was an absurd amount of runway in my opinion. Of course, Eric knew precisely what he was talking about. My confidence alone wasn't going to get a team together. We had to find players who had basketball in their blood. Process is nothing without the right people.

If you haven't won a national championship, you really don't know how to win a national championship. I see that now that we have won three. Prior to that achievement, you have zero notion of what it takes. It takes more than talent. It takes more than luck. It takes more than timing. It requires a village of folks who have synergy and a shared immutable faith that a title is within reach.

I'll say it again, process is nothing without the right people.

Parents must have belief. Boyfriends or girlfriends, they must have belief. Trainers, nutritionists, pals they work out with, they must have belief. Everybody, soup to nuts, even amid a subpar year, must believe and row full throttle in the direction of that conviction.

That part is easy for me. Give me a year in which we go sub–five hundred, you're still not going to make me dwell on losing. You're not going to make me lose faith. Sometimes you can get into a situation where you want to settle. Or tell yourself, *Well, that's the best we could do*. Not on my watch. On my watch, we fight. We do the Ted Lasso. We believe.

As we continued to reboot the program at South Carolina, in every meeting with potential players, I'd ask, "Do you love basketball?" The response had to be a resounding "*yes!*" If it wasn't, we didn't need to explore any further. If I had to squeeze out a "sure" for the love of basketball, I knew they were not going to be willing and able to do what we asked of them.

There were players we went after who wanted us to pay them under the table. That was an instant pass. We knew other programs were finding workarounds, but I would not and could not. I'd be ashamed of doing that. I would lose every game, I would lose my job before I'd resort to shady tactics or compromise my integrity. That meant our USC recruiting messaging had to be better than easy promises. Luckily, we had the right mix of coaches who worked their collective butts off.

There's nobody who's going to go harder than Boyer. Nobody. Carla strategized twenty-four hours a day. Nikki was a tireless recruiter, a tireless warrior. Then I brought in Darius Taylor, who was with me at Temple. I met him through USA Basketball. Darius could handle anything. Between us, there wasn't a task too big or too small. Nothing slipped through the cracks. We decided, simply, we were not going to fail.

After the third year, finally, we'd signed up a team where 80 percent of our players were basketball fanatics. That's when things started trending in the right direction. By the fourth year our team was ready to compete at a high level. Not NCAA high, but notches above what we were able to make happen in the first three seasons.

What creates momentum in a program is being steadfast. You need foresight. When you're not getting huge results, you have to spot minute improvements and build on those. Most important, you must be clear-eyed. Denial is a hell of a drug. And has no place in a successful program.

Part of what that meant was I had to be brutally honest with myself and how I interacted with my players and my larger team. I needed to examine how I was relating to different people and how they responded to me. I wasn't in Philly anymore. Just like when I was at the University of Virginia, I was going to need to adapt.

To that end, I began making it a priority to personally get to know each of our players. Something I've done ever since. That doesn't mean I have a strong relationship with every member of the team, because that may not be what they want. But I'm available. I'm open. I'm willing. The root of success in any league is the ability to connect with each other. If your players feel your willingness to see them, that's the ticket.

When I was a young coach trying to establish myself, I didn't think I should socialize with or hang around with my players. I wanted to establish boundaries. And if I'm honest,

I was still in many ways the same reserved person I had been as a child and in college. Staying private and keeping to myself was my comfort zone. I didn't account for the fact that the players might want to hang around with me. Or that bonding off the court would improve relationships on the court.

Back then, a couple of members of the team kept dropping by my house. They were sweet, easy to be with. We made each other laugh. They called on me to help them navigate rough patches. Teach them life skills. Everything from job-interview etiquette to why you shouldn't wear maxi pads during games. They relied on me for guidance, and in turn, they changed how I viewed my role as coach. I learned I could be less standoffish, more accessible. That I was valuable as a mentor off the court. That *all* aspects of my life held value, not simply the parts centered around ball.

To make it work at South Carolina I needed to double down on that accessibility. That applied to our players and our fans. The AD told me explicitly that he needed me more "out front," meaning, I had to be visible in the public spotlight.

Socially, I had to get used to certain things, such as the molasses pace of the South, and the fact that every conversation lasts twice as long as it does in the North and inevitably contains way TMI. Other novelties I came to accept, such as being called "ma'am." (That one took me a while.)

To expand our program, I began holding fan and local press forums, asking what they wanted to see from us. We incorporated the feedback and made changes, such as offering assigned seats at Colonial Life Arena and more behind-the-scenes access to players. I called in favors from WNBA players and Olympians. Used my connections to add a bit of shine to the program. The aim was to turn our arena into the hottest ticket in town. Grow our program externally as we built it internally.

We instituted theme words for each season, which became tent poles for the whole community to rally around. Sacrifice. Be the Change. The Show. One. We Are. What Matters. DNA. Uncommon.

We added a special club for our fans called the G-Hive (shamelessly borrowing from Beyoncé's BeyHive). We socialized with our fan base, treating the G-Hive like royalty. Bringing them in for practices, scheduling Zooms with the players, Facebook Lives. We made them feel valued, because they were. One fan shared that his grandmother told him, "Treat people good, they'll treat you better." I tell you, we adopted that motto full stop. As a result of all that outreach, today we have eleven thousand season ticket holders. Our arena sells out in minutes.

All to say, the foundation of our Gamecocks success was built on the philosophy that process principles are less critical than *people* principles. Because once you have the people—fans, players, community—on board, the basketball is the easy part. Anyone can teach themselves how to X and O. Reaching the individuals on your team, in your stands—that's where the magic happens.

After those rough pioneering years, we improved every season. Then, in 2017, nearly a decade after I started the job, we won our first national championship against Mississippi State.

The year prior, 2016, in South Dakota, we got our ass beat by Syracuse in the Sweet 16. I gathered the players after that and said, "How you feel right now? You never want to feel this way again." It lit a fire under our collective butts.

In reality, we were in many ways underdogs in 2017. We'd lost to Missouri. We weren't gelling like I wanted. As we headed off to Stockton, California, for regionals, it was time to lock in. We knew we wouldn't be back home till after the Final Four. Staying on the road that many weeks, in a place so remote from home, our players came to rely on each other even more. It was a bit like Olympic training camp, where you're sequestered with your teammates at the exclusion of all the typical, everyday distractions. When you're always together, no separate corners, more bonding naturally occurs. I saw that happening with our team. Which was good.

Less good was the fact that being in California cut down our fan base. It was a long haul from Columbia. The USC men's team was also playing in the tournament. Many supporters had to choose which team to support. In the end, our young ladies, who were used to playing for around thirteen thousand fans screaming for them, found themselves in an arena with thirty-one hundred people barely screaming at all.

I remember worrying that we'd already played Mississippi State twice. We beat them in the regular season and in the SEC tournament. Matching with them again for the national title was nuts. Statistically, you don't usually beat the same team multiple times in a season. But for us, that year, the third time was the charm.

It feels like yesterday. Fundamentally, basketball is a game of runs. In the third quarter, Mississippi was within five points, and I sensed they had one run left in them. During our time-out,

I was honest with my team. I told them in a calm, measured voice, "If we don't stop their next run, we're going to lose." Everyone was exhausted, the wear and tear of the season obvious on their faces. I appealed to their emotions, saying the fourth quarter would come down to who wanted it most.

The time-out ended, and we put our hands in together. Inside, I was a bundle of nerves. I hid my feelings, pacing the sideline as my team battled. When a player caught my eye, I flashed a reassuring look. I knew my projecting confidence would make them feel they could do it. Sure enough, we went on our own run.

By the 2:52 mark we found ourselves up by ten points. Our team had dug deep. It was statistically impossible for Mississippi State to catch us. I only had to stay composed a few heartbeats more.

At the two-second mark, I walked toward the opposing bench to congratulate their coach on a hard-fought game. As I made my way to him, I was aware of the magnitude of what we had just accomplished. We were about to win our first national championship and take our place as the best in the country.

When the final buzzer sounded, hometown hero A'ja Wilson dropped to her knees and wept, a towel over her head. In a postgame interview, she thanked me for being honest with the players, for my loyalty. That meant the world to me. It took ten years, but I'd managed to shape my team into the champions I knew they could be, while also honing myself into the best version of a coach I could be.

I'm currently finishing my seventeenth season at South Carolina. These days, I want my players to be leaders, I want them to have opinions, I want them to know what they want, I want them to feel important. I remain an old-school coach, but it's all about being respectful and receiving respect back. People before process.

When it comes to being a coach, I'm not done with it quite yet. Look how long Pat Summitt was at Tennessee. Geno Auriemma is still dominating at UConn. Why would any coach leave if there's not a good reason? Each year provides me an opportunity to wrestle unique obstacles. Because of that and for so many other reasons, coaching has become my second skin.

Over the years, just as I have matured, South Carolina has grown to allow me to be my authentic self. That doesn't mean they agree with everything I say. Trust me, they do not. But they know where my loyalty lies. I treat people right. I want to win. At the same time, if I need to let folks know where I stand, I will. The beautiful thing is that there is space for that.

The great unspoken truth about coaching is that for all you give, you get it back tenfold. It's funny, many of those players from my initial terrible, no-good seasons have come back to watch USC games. They'll come up to me and say, "Now I see what you were trying to get us to do!" We'll have a laugh and a hug. It's a beautiful thing to see the evolution of our program.

I can't pinpoint the exact day I knew I'd made the right choice moving to South Carolina. It's hard to tell because I didn't lift my head up until we started winning. I can say this: When I survey the crowds at our games, my spirit soars in a way it never had at my other coaching gigs. It goes beyond the basketball court; it goes beyond our team.

The Black community here who attend our games, before I arrived, some of them had never set foot on campus. At the grocery store, the hair salon—you have to stop and listen to South Carolinians because they like to tell you their business—strangers approach me and share that they didn't want to come onto our campus, because not so long ago they or members of their families were not allowed to be there because of the color of their skin. They couldn't even walk through. They had to walk *around*.

I hear stories like that and I understand that what I'm building in South Carolina is worlds bigger than basketball.

Our fans come together because sports create common ground. Black, white, Republican, Democrat, Independent, our fans are from every walk of life. During the games, they set all those personal differences aside. They cheer and high-five. They find themselves gaining friendships they didn't expect.

My existence at USC breaks down barriers. I believe, as I sit here, it was divined for me to take this job. Out of all the places I could have gone as a young, Black, successful professional, I chose to come to South Carolina. Since I have, our program has been a unifier. When you look at the fans at our games, it's the most diverse congregation in the state.

When we won our second national championship in 2022, we beat UConn. They are the gold standard in women's basketball. Geno and his program, they've been the go-to for excellence for a very, very long time. Defeating them validated us in everybody's eyes.

After that victory, there was a parade down Main Street in Columbia. I was in a convertible. The first parade in 2017, we rode in a bus, looking down from up high, doing the pageant wave. This time, we were at ground level, and the crowd went wild.

We were engulfed by fans. They swarmed the car, shouting at the top of their lungs, "We love you!" or "You're the GOAT!" So many people cheering, pointing at me, and thanking me for what I'd done. I had my Sharpie out, signing autographs as we inched along the route. Some fans were crying.

The whole event was an out-of-body experience. Everything that was happening landed on a level far deeper than winning. It showed me that what we're achieving with our program, with our success, is nothing less than inviting Black people to feel like South Carolina is their program, too. That they have a place at the table. Ownership in our wins. My players and I make our community proud. And I'm super proud of that.

God works in mysterious ways. I was meant to be at South Carolina. It was my path. Not to win championships, but to bring people together.

To change the processes that leave people out.

Know Your Worth

In 2021, women's basketball, like everything else on the planet, was white-knuckling it through the Covid bubble. That was back when everything felt dark, when we were thankful for a walk, for a breath of fresh air.

At the time, I was focused on not just South Carolina basketball but the NCAA tournament and women's basketball more broadly. I wanted to keep both hope and the sport alive. Give the players and the fans a reason to feel good about something, a spot to park their worries and woes.

March arrived and the sixty-four women's teams gathered in San Antonio, Texas, gearing up for the tournament. All was business as usual until the eighteenth, when the Oregon Ducks forward Sedona Prince released the now infamous thirty-eight-second video on her socials, where she compared the training facilities for the women with those in Indiana for the men. The difference was stark.

The men's teams had a fully tricked-out gym that resembled a fitness club, whereas the women's teams had a sad yoga mat and a single weight stand with a few dinky hand weights. It was a worse setup than you'd find at a cheap motel.

After showing the side by side, Sedona said into the camera, "If you're not upset about this problem, then you're a part of it."

The images and what they revealed about the baseline investment in women's sports versus men's sparked an instant firestorm. It went viral. Steph Curry retweeted the video to his millions of followers with the comment "Wow! Come on now!" Soon talk shows and news programs were airing the clip on their networks. Sexism in sports became the chatter of the country.

For us on the inside, it wasn't as if we didn't know inequity existed. For the longest time it's been ingrained in women to just be thankful for what we have. Appreciate the crumbs. But the simple message of the video penetrated the noise. Within days, the post had been viewed more than thirteen million times.

The glaring spotlight and subsequent media coverage lit up other inequities between the men's and women's programs. Everything from catering to lodging to medical care to swag bags was compared and shown to be a version of the same unbalanced story. We were left marinating in the fresh exposure of the numerous ways the NCAA (to say nothing of other sports leagues) has routinely treated female players as second-class citizens.

The negative press created a frenzy as the people in charge engaged in the age-old practice of CYA. Folks started asking questions and pointing fingers. For my part, I fired off a letter to my fellow coaches. Made some sharp social media posts. Held Zoom meetings. I amplified the disparity and called for accountability as much as I could.

The NCAA president, Mark Emmert, hemmed and hawed, but when the controversy didn't die down, he commissioned an external review. The results found the contracts and revenue distribution, as well as the internal culture, had perpetuated and normalized gender inequities between the men's and women's tournaments. Women athletes were unsurprised. But we were glad the data was out there in black-and-white. Maybe now something could be done to balance the scales.

When I returned home after the competition, it was time for me to renegotiate my contract with South Carolina. As I was considering my ask, it hit me. Wait a second—I'm out here fighting on a national level to even the playing field between women's and men's basketball, but I'm not advocating for the same at home. It was a welcome epiphany.

With Sedona's video and the feverish media coverage of the report that followed, the debate around equal investment and valuing what women bring to sports was never more front and center. I decided if I was going to be a role model for gender equity, I needed to ask for what I deserved. Equal pay and nothing less. The time was long overdue. The day had come to put my mouth where my money was.

I grew up watching my mom stand up for what's right. She used to embarrass us kids because she couldn't let a wrong go unnoticed. No matter who was involved, it didn't matter. It could have been the president of the United States. She would've spoken out. She would march over and let anyone know when they weren't acting right. I'd stand next to her, trying to shrink myself, mortified. Cut to now, and I realize I am made that same way. The apple does not fall far from the calling-out-injustice tree. I am, above all, my mother's child.

Now, I'm not knee-jerk. I will pause and give thought to an issue. Sit with my feelings a day or two. If it bothers me after that, then I know I need to say something. When it came to my salary, I did a little investigating. I looked at what the men's basketball coach was making. I knew what I was making. Then I saw his raises and compared them to mine. I came away from my research thinking there was something seriously wrong here.

Our track records were not the same. He'd made it to the Final Four once. I understood asking for equal pay was a risk. I was proposing something that had never been granted before. But I believed my case was strong. And more important, I was willing to walk away if I lost.

I don't coach for money. I don't do anything just for money. Money doesn't drive me. Relationships do. Achievement does. While I'm at the University of South Carolina as head coach of the women's basketball team, I want us to be dominant. My loyalty is to my players and my program. Money is secondary.

That said, when you see what your male counterparts are earning while not reaching anywhere near the level of success you're having, it is a tough pill to swallow.

Much of this is, of course, a systemic problem that has devalued women and women's sports for decades. The balances are tilted in favor of men, regardless of whether they win, net higher ratings, or fill stadium seats. Even when women's teams dominate, the players make less money. Same goes for the coaches. This is true even down to bonuses. When men renegotiate, they are doing so within different parameters, with higher limits and fewer excuses from the powers that be for why they shouldn't be rewarded with more money. I believe everyone's bonuses should reflect the success that they're having. It's quite simple. But sometimes people don't value others' success as equal.

My mother expected me to do the right thing, to walk in my truth. But she wasn't naive. She knew the score. She'd warn that I needed to be courageous enough to stand in the ring and take the hits that would inevitably come.

I would soon find out if I was.

When I began the salary negotiation process, I understood the debate was not going to be easy sledding. I asked my agent to stand down. He wasn't thrilled. He wanted to fight the fight, which, if I were him, I would've wanted, too. He'd been in my corner long before we were at the stage of equal pay. But this cause was too important to not arm myself with every tool I could to prevail.

I hired a local lawyer, Butch Bowers, who personally knew the decision-makers. All the power players, the people on the board of trustees, the movers and shakers in Columbia. He understood when you are asking for equal pay, it's not going to be a quick one-on-one with the athletic director.

Most critically, Butch believed in the argument. When someone believes in a cause, they don't have a hard time fighting for it. This is not to suggest the fight was easy. It was not. I mean, we're in a small southern city; if somebody's going to make a move like this, everybody's going to have a say or an opinion. My salary soon became the talk of the town.

The conversation began in April. It was push. It was pull. It was "I don't have any more money." The back-and-forth strung out to October. All throughout, the AD and I would be business as usual, reviewing the schedule or discussing team matters. We have a good relationship. I'm able to be straight with him. Sometimes the contract negotiation would slide into the chat.

I can remember him calling my bluff: "You're going to leave all of that money on the table?" In his mind, my normal raise should have been plenty. What's a few extra dollars?

Time and again I explained it wasn't about the dollars. It was about the principle of the matter. I can't be leading the charge nationally for gender equity and not getting that back home, where I'm many times more successful than my male counterpart. Nothing against Coach Frank Martin. I have endless respect for Frank. But to give Frank an automatic pay increase versus what I was given didn't seem fair or right.

That detail really got under my skin. The fact that the male coach's built-in pay increases, regardless of job execution, were much higher. How is somebody who wasn't achieving at the pace of our program receiving more of a pay bump? I'm at the top of the SEC. Was I not supposed to get a raise for my success? You're not going to give the national championship coach a raise? I just couldn't wrap my head around that. It was, in a way, embarrassing to me.

I don't doubt the board interrogated Butch: "Why do you think she deserves this?" Paying me equally drives up the whole market. No one wants to be the person who sets that pattern in motion, even if it's the right thing to do. I wasn't oblivious to the dynamics our AD was subject to. I felt for him. But what was fair remained.

More than once I've heard from athletic directors that they consider women's basketball a money pit. When those people argue, "Well, you're a non-revenue-producing sport," I show them the receipts.

Under my stewardship to that date, the South Carolina program captured five SEC regular-season championships, seven SEC tournament titles, four Final Fours, three NCAA national championships, seven Sweet 16 appearances, five SEC Player of the Year awards, and five SEC Freshman of the Year awards. In 2024, I guided the team to a perfect 38–0 season. I've been awarded SEC Coach of the Year seven times.

As a result, we have the highest game attendance in the country. We've set records the past nine years in a row. Somebody's paying for those tickets. Somebody's keeping those concession stands open. That's revenue producing.

Over the past seven years, I've been the most successful coach in the country. Donors give because I'm here. We're winning natties. You're getting a free marketing campaign off our swag equity. We're brand lift for the whole school, to say nothing of brand lift for the whole sport. Enrollment is up. Partly because these students watched us win championships.

Young women are making decisions to come to South Carolina because they see me speak up, they see the product on the floor, and that makes them proud and eager to be a part of South Carolina. We are the difference maker in some decisions. What is that? A hundred-thousand-dollar commitment per student if they stay four years. Don't tell me we don't produce revenue.

Every negotiation process that I've had, I've heard this acronym: FMV. Fair market value. To which I ask, who's my competition? Whom are you comparing me to? I get you can go to Geno and say he's got eleven national championships with UConn. You could go to LSU's Kim Mulkey and say she's got four. But I have three. And I'm different from the two of them. The value I bring to USC is unique. I've done my research. I have the figures. The university knows the number of impressions they net from me. How far and wide my reach is in service of the school. Where I move the needle for visibility.

As the discussions dragged on, I tried to get our AD to understand that all of the above notwithstanding, granting equal pay would be a win-win, whether he believed it or not. It would be a win for me and him, and the university, and women, and the whole grand scheme of basketball. Hell, it would be a win for the country. We'd be an example of living up to the national ideals of opportunity and equality for all.

Times have changed from the old days. Check out the last ten years of the sport. We are not in the same place that we were when it comes to how women's basketball is perceived. You can't measure us with the old metrics.

Years ago, if you wanted to watch a women's game, the choice was one game, once a week. Now everybody tunes in to multiple games. Last year, the NCAA announced a new contract with ESPN for $920 million to air collegiate championships. In it, they doubled the value of the women's games to $65 million. Which I call a start.

We in the business know women's basketball has value. Immeasurable value really, if you factor in what it means for girls to be able to see themselves in our players. Women athletes are among the most highly admired people in the country. Polls repeatedly show this. They are terrific brand ambassadors. They inspire fierce loyalty and trust.

When I was younger it was rare to see women athletes in media. Maybe during the Olympics. The women I did watch compete inspired me like nothing else. Jackie Joyner-Kersee, Serena Williams, Teresa Edwards, Flo-Jo, Steffi Graf. I devoured any coverage I could find. It was a case of you didn't have much, so what you had, you cherished, and it may have been nothing to anyone else, but it was enormously meaningful to you.

As I grew older, I began to register the lack of wider representation. Less than 5 percent of all sports media coverage is devoted to women. And now here I am—representing. As my mother would advise, those of us who can fight the fight should.

I'm not saying go out there and risk it all. Tackle the small battles. Build toward bigger ones. Which is where we find ourselves in the conversation around women's athletics.

I think what's come to light, and should have been exposed a long time ago, is the false assumption that fans aren't interested or don't care or won't watch women's sports. The math doesn't math. It's been proven in multiple instances with the WNBA and March Madness, with women's soccer and hockey, and with women's Olympic sports, the product they're selling is as good as or better than the men's side.

Women's basketball specifically is a hotbed. WNBA game attendance is on the rise. Television ratings are higher than ever. Now is the time to scale up, invest in us, and watch what happens.

Men's pro basketball is a billion-dollar business. If people invested in women's basketball like they do men's, we could generate a whole lot of profit. Less than 1 percent of sponsorship dollars goes to women's sports. I don't understand the resistance. Isn't the money that we would make as green? Why wouldn't you want to make as much profit as possible? It's not like our earnings would take any money *away* from the men's pot.

Open the books and let's review the ledger. The WNBA raised $75 million in its first-ever funding round in 2022. After which, the league was valued at $1 billion. That indicates the WNBA is marketable. Hopefully some of that $75 million ends up in the players' pockets. Currently the WNBA is a place where there's only a limited number of jobs. The WNBA is expanding from twelve teams to fifteen by 2026, which is a positive step. But great players are still at home right now doing nothing or forced to travel overseas to play. So, we keep pushing.

It's not often you get a chance to control the narrative when it comes to what you are worth. Women, as a rule, are told. That's just the fact of the matter.

I think that's another reason I stuck to my convictions on equal pay. I was tired of being told.

All of this makes me think about a film I watched called *Worth*, about the victims of 9/11 and their families' fight for compensation. It was based on the true story of lawyers who had developed a formula for what each person's payout should be, based on their perceived "worth." What was a fireman worth? A janitor? A CEO? Predictably, the proposed argument was that the tragic deaths of wealthier individuals were considered more significant. Which is obviously nonsense. But it is a window into what our society deems is of value, and how far we still must go to correct those ingrained perceptions.

I walk every single day. My route takes me through campus. There's not one day that goes by that a person doesn't come up to me. Boys, girls, adults. They want a selfie. They tell me how much they love me and how much I mean to them. How much their parents adore me. Many of the female students thank me for what I do for women. I hear it time and time again.

I'm uncomfortable sharing these things (though I will say those interactions are lovely and a real boost to my self-confidence). The point is, young adults are watching and learning. They see how I'm treated, and they imagine their own futures and the treatment that waits for them.

That's why my being paid equitably goes far beyond the numbers. If someone with my achievements can't demand equity, who can? This battle isn't about me. It's about everyone who comes after me.

I'm happy to say that after many months and considerable pressure from my lawyer and other allies, the university and the athletic department did the right thing and granted me equitable pay.

Our AD was a brave one for doing it. I applaud him. I know it's not easy for a board to announce they're going to pay their women's basketball coach $22.4 million. I can imagine him walking into the room with all the other ADs shaking their heads and clucking, "Man, why'd you go and do that?" I appreciate that it was tricky for the board because they set a formal precedent. My getting equal pay doesn't happen in a vacuum. It starts a chain reaction.

Which was the entire goal.

I'm in it to win it for everybody, but for women especially. I know we can pull our own weight. I want to shout from the rooftops, "Bet on us!" Do I deserve equal pay? Yes. Yes, I do. But the real battle is bigger than any one person or team. It's the campaign to be seen and treated as equals on all fronts.

Sometimes when you're fighting the fight and victory happens, you're like, *Oh.* Your mind jumps right to asking, *What's the next thing?* What else can I fight for? It's like, okay, that's done with, on to the next battle.

After a national championship, when the last buzzer sounds, I'm instantly tired. I'm relieved. There's elation, but with it exhaustion. They say the body keeps the score. When you've been pushing whatever boulder up a hill for months and months, the body is spent.

Winning pay equity was like that. It was a relief. They did the honorable thing. But I was beat. I knew there would be more fights to come. My mother taught me that the struggle to know, to show your worth is constant. But what choice is there?

When I consider the young women on my team, what I ask of them—to do things the right way, not to cheat themselves or cut corners—when I say they can climb as high as they want, be all that they want, that has to mean something. I can't be in the business of empty promises.

Which is why I speak out.

I can't ask them to stand up for themselves if I'm sitting down. I can't encourage them to use their voice to effect change if I'm only willing to whisper.

I'm a softhearted person, believe it or not. I give people the benefit of the doubt more times than not. Sometimes that means I don't get everything that I deserve, and I don't get everything that I want. Most times, I'm okay with that. But there are other times when I can't let things go. When injustice keeps me up at night.

We need more advocates who believe in women's sports to fight for women's sports. The hard truth is there are many ADs and university presidents who quietly whisper, "Let's just get rid of all the girls' programs." Even when the women's teams draw record television ratings. (Our 2024 title game against Iowa drew 18.9 million viewers, outpacing the men's title game by more than 3 million to become the most-watched basketball matchup, college or pro, since 2019.)

To those college authorities I ask, "Don't you consider the women in your life? The girls in your life?" To hold one of us down is to hold us all back. To erase our value is to suggest to every woman, you have no right to believe in your own significance.

The solution lies in more cases like mine. If I don't fight for my value, few others have a chance. I would have been okay win or lose. But most women don't have that luxury. It was a moral imperative for me to raise this case. I believe all of us who have any standing, any privilege should be the ones climbing out on the limbs of insisting on social change, because our fall would be cushioned.

I don't mind fighting. I feel like I'm constantly fighting something. Social injustice, pay inequity, disparities in the treatment of women's and men's collegiate and professional athletics, intolerance. I mean, I've been fighting my whole entire life. It's second nature to me. Truthfully, I welcome it. I need opposition in my life. It sharpens me like a blade against a grindstone. It winnows my focus to the task at hand.

What makes all the battling easier is knowing every time I stand up, I'm honoring my mom. If I witness injustice and turn my head, that makes me culpable. If I witness someone being treated unfairly and I do nothing, I'm participating in the wrongdoing. I have my platform, and I refuse to take it for granted.

There's a Title IX attorney named Janet Judge who tours the country speaking to different coaches and athletic departments. Recently she shared that a lot of her speeches are about me. I forced the decision-makers of women's basketball to step up. I'm the highest-paid Black female coach ever. Janet told me I pushed the conversations around equality forward. That my voice matters to people.

I see these young people and know that my fight is laying the foundation for all they dream to build. I never forget the world is watching.

That's the thing about knowing your worth. The value in that isn't in what you reap. It's in what you sow.

Look, Sound, Feel

For as long as I can remember, Philadelphia 76er Allen "the Answer" Iverson has been an inspiration to me. He spent fourteen seasons in the NBA as a point guard, starting in 1996. Punching above his weight every game.

At six feet tall, 165 pounds, Iverson was small for the NBA. It never held him back. What he lacked in size he made up for in swagger and style. I sparked to his ball handling first. When I observed him play, it was as if he was everywhere all at once. He carried the ball with brazen finesse. I'd watch him pass and marvel at how he was able to exploit every opening. He was also a clutch scorer. When he stepped onto the court, it was as if he had something to prove. I could relate.

His combination of hunger and heart spoke to me. I mean,

all the kids coming of age in the projects identified with AI. He was like us. He was for us. The passion that he bled. The audacity of his game. AI didn't play by the rules expected of young Black men in the NBA during those years. He didn't kowtow or stay quiet to make himself palatable to certain audiences. He was one of the first players who refused to "shut up and dribble." Iverson was an example of somebody we could watch and say to ourselves, *If he can do it, so can I.*

In 1993, Iverson was arrested. He was seventeen years old. The arrest followed an altercation at a bowling alley in Virginia, his home state. A fight had erupted between a group of white and Black kids. Afterward, he and three of his friends, all Black, were the only people jailed. Iverson was not offered bond, a legal prohibition usually reserved for murderers. Later, he was convicted of a felony.

When a videotape eventually surfaced showing Iverson exiting the bowling alley shortly after the fighting began, he'd already spent four months at the Newport News City Farm correctional facility.

The Virginia Court of Appeals ultimately overturned the conviction in 1995 for insufficient evidence, but the example had been made, and the damage had been done. The prison sentence forced AI to complete his senior year of high school at a school for "at-risk" students, instead of competing where he'd played before, at Bethel. Thankfully, he was recruited by Georgetown University based on his prior three years of play.

AI's lived reality mirrored that of so many of my friends and neighbors. His success in the face of that reality was a beacon. His existence was resistance. These days I'm proud to call him a friend.

He told me he was nervous when we first met. Apparently, I was his favorite player while I was at Virginia. He watched me on television, just as I'd watched him while he was in Philly. We have a unique bond from playing in each other's home states. He tells folks I'm his favorite women's basketball player of all time, a compliment that humbles me.

Along with AI, I really identify with four-time NBA All-Star point guard Maurice (Mo) Cheeks. Today I'd have to say he's my number one player of all time. For eleven seasons with the 76ers, Mo represented substance and professionalism, but he was lethal on the court, ending his NBA career as the league's all-time leader in steals. He's one of only seven former Sixers to have his number retired.

As a person, Mo was reserved. As a point guard, he was the consummate giver and a steadying influence. He prioritized setting up his teammates for success. His unselfish approach was devastatingly effective. In the mix with legends such as Dr. J and Moses Malone, Mo acted as the glue. I considered him the unsung hero on my beloved team. The opposite of flashy, he deployed his talents like water, flowing around any obstacle.

As a young girl, I didn't have the edge to be the next AI, but I convinced myself that I could be the next Mo Cheeks, if I just got good enough. That's the thing about imagination. It gives you an opportunity to dream, no matter how outlandish your dreams are. I knew everything about the Sixers. After Mo took us to a 1983 championship, I thought I was the next point guard up. I tried to model my game after him.

I put in the work. Hell, I craved the work. Still, it didn't take long before I realized I wasn't going to be the next Maurice Cheeks. Or any player I admired, for that matter. I could study plays and borrow technique and emulate style and draft off their inventiveness and follow their example, but at the end of the day, I had to cut my own path.

When you're raised in North Philly, there are certain characteristics and abilities you inherit that come with the territory. You're always going to be aware of your surroundings. You're going to have an innate sense of when something is about to go off. You're going to know whom you can mess with, and whom to stay away from. You're going to be able to size someone up with just a glance. The education North Philly unsparingly provides is one emphasizing vigilance, acuity, confidence, and courage. Put simply, you stay awake, and you trust your gut.

As an adult, I call this life hack "look, sound, feel."

It's the system I use to assess everything I come across. How does something, look, sound, feel in the moment? What are my instincts telling me? I consider it my North Philly superpower.

I wouldn't be the same player or coach had I been born in any other city, that I know for sure. From the beginning, a lot of what I did on the court was based on my intuition. My approach to the game, my judgment of character, my ability to anticipate actions and outcomes, all were grounded in look, sound, feel. Another person might possess the same abilities, but chances are they would not have been tested as early or as often.

Those early lessons have also translated to how I lead my

teams. If I'm at practice and I feel something hinky, I'll stop and adjust on the fly. It's part of my creative touch for the game. Very much like being a point guard, there's an organized chaos. There may be breakneck activity in motion, but I know exactly what's happening out of the corner of my eye. When I'm coaching, I keep myriad options and executions in my head at the same time. I spot the deficiencies. I figure it out in real time. Like Jay-Z, I just mic it.

The same method works for my own emotional processing. If I have a thorny dilemma, or a worrying situation, I take a walk, clear my head. How do things look, sound, and feel with some breathing room? Not every thought needs to be organized. Some people write strategy down, type out the ABCs, the pro and con lists. My approach is more like jazz, fluid and alive. A swirl of moving parts that coalesce into an unexpected swell of music. I don't necessarily defer to my instincts all the time, but I never ignore them.

I recall a workout during the Olympic trials in 1996. My teammates were mostly from the South and Midwest, with one player from Los Angeles. I was the only person from a big East Coast city. They would always tell me I was different, that there was something in the way I carried myself that stood out. One afternoon, we were doing a competition scrimmage. Our coach, Tara VanDerveer, separated us into two groups. Somehow, my squad kept losing.

The punishment for losing was running laps. By our third loss, I was convinced Tara was favoring the other group. Each scrimmage we ran, I grew more and more certain. Now, if I lose fairly, I can accept the consequences. But this was clearly unmerited. And that's when my look, sound, feel kicked off. My North Philly spidey senses were tingling.

I noticed the coaches kept huddling together, which didn't usually happen during drills. I called the assistant coach over and pressed her: What was going on? She didn't answer, gave me a weird look and a shrug.

After my group's fourth straight loss, the winning group began teasing us. That went over like a lead balloon. The women on my team began mumbling under their breath. One glance at their faces and I knew they were fuming but afraid to say anything out loud. The vibe was getting tense.

Six straight losses later, I'd seen and felt enough.

"I don't care what you do, you're not going to break us!" I yelled.

My teammates took notice. Seven losses, eight losses, the hits kept coming. When we lined up to sprint yet again, I sped from the line, shouting even louder.

"You can cheat if you want to, but you will not break us! We will not break! *We will not break!*"

I made sure to lead the pack. My lungs burning, I stayed out front, screaming loud enough for everyone in the building to hear. My teammates joined the chorus, following my lead. We banded together, chanting as a unit, "We will not break! We will not break!"

From that moment on, it was us against them, with me leading the charge.

Two things happened that practice. I recognized the look, sound, feel antennae I'd developed in my youth were what led me to notice what was happening, call it out, and rally the troops. And second, as my coaches later disclosed, that drill was a psychological one meant to identify the group's natural leader. They created undue duress to see who would emerge and step up. I was one of the youngest and smallest players on the team, but there I was, stepping up and emerging as the voice of the team. North Philly superpower activated!

I've played for numerous coaches in my career. Those who are strictly positive. Those who are unerringly methodical. Those who are creative.

I've been led by a coach who allowed me to make mistakes and talked me through those mistakes. I've been coached by someone who pretty much rolled the ball out and said, "Do what you need to do to create your magic." I've had coaches who played head games, those who thought outside of the box, those who beat players down to build them up, and those who just did the beating-down part. I've taken all those experiences and extracted what works for me. Through it all, look, sound, feel remains bedrock. It's the core of who I am as a coach.

Unlike most of my peers, I've rarely set concrete goals. I've never felt comfortable declaring I want to do this or that. Maybe that's weird. Most successful people set goals for themselves. I knew I wanted to win a national championship and a gold medal. Other than that, I've let life guide me to where I'm supposed to be. (Now, I wouldn't tell that to a young person. That's too open-ended. Instead I'd say to concentrate on something you love and aim your arrow there.)

Of course, competitive me, once I got into coaching, I aspired to do it at the highest level. I had two opportunities as an assistant coach with Team USA. Under the late great

Anne Donovan in 2008, and then when Geno Auriemma welcomed me onto the 2016 Olympics staff.

With USA Basketball, you need to let them know you have interest in coaching. You don't go from being a good college coach to boom, you're an Olympic coach! You put in your time leading the younger teams, knowing the Olympic committee is watching you, observing how you deal with players and situations that aren't nice or easy. You climb your way up to the national team.

When I was selected head coach for the 2020 Tokyo Olympics—oh my God, was that a different feeling. I don't believe I got the job automatically because I was a part of two Olympic staffs. I think I was selected because of my additional service as a player, along with my past coaching of the Pan American Games and other international tournaments.

The pressure was intense from day one. Directing players who are pros in their day jobs is a whole different animal from managing college kids. They were the best in the sport, but I was calling the shots and carrying the responsibility for netting gold. All the weight was on me.

When our team began playing together at Team USA's training camp in Las Vegas, we lost. *Twice.* We lost a game to the WNBA All-Star team. And another to the Australians. After that, I lost sleep.

I couldn't unwind for days. I went into a headspace of *Well, shit.* The unexpected defeats spurred negative media buzz. I was the first Black head coach leading an Olympic women's team. I felt my back against the wall.

The last time Team USA lost gold in the Olympics was in

the 1992 semifinals. I couldn't be the reason that happened again. I found myself haunted by our equally shocking loss in the 2006 world championship semifinals when I was an assistant coach. In my head, I was spiraling.

I watched more film. I gave myself additional self-talks. I needed to create a new path, but I couldn't figure out how to pivot. It was a lonely place. There's only one head coach of an Olympic basketball team. And it was me. And the team wasn't gelling.

I chose not to reach out to my old coach Tara VanDerveer. She'd been encouraging and supportive of my appointment, but I decided not to call for advice. She'd only suggest I coach her way. I didn't hit up Geno either. Or any of the coaches who had educated me. My choice was to take it all in and deal with the facts on the ground my way. I needed to return to my instincts. Look, sound, feel.

I got still and quiet and drilled down on the essentials. There were a lot of unknowns in coaching my first Olympic team. I needed to uncover what was known to me. I began by figuring out who the starters should be. I knew the players, their skill sets. It was virtually the same team from the gold-winning 2016 Games. Sue Bird, Breanna Stewart, Diana Taurasi, Brittney Griner.

It dawned on me that maybe that was the root of my dilemma. I was pressuring myself not to screw anything up, because that configuration had it going on. They were used to each other. They'd built chemistry. They were proven.

Olympic newbie A'ja Wilson was a rising star. As she'd come from my South Carolina team, I had an ease and comfort with her. She was my safe space. Look, sound, feel was a love language we shared.

Those two games we fumbled, I didn't play A'ja a whole lot. I was giving respect to the older players. It was A'ja's debut Games, and I wanted her to get used to things. After the back-to-back losses, I decided we ain't getting used to not winning.

I decided to add A'ja to the starting lineup, along with Sue, Diana, Stew, and Brittney. That meant I'd need to bump veteran center Tina Charles. My decision was not without controversy. I spoke to Tina, asked her, How would you feel about not starting? Would it impact your ability to help us win a gold medal?

"I'm a player first," she responded. Meaning, I'm going to do what I need to do for the team.

It was a tough conversation. But necessary. Honesty is how you respect players and what they bring to the table. Tina was a pro. She was a two-time Olympian at that point. She knew we were there to figure out the best recipe for victory.

Once I elevated A'ja, it wasn't so much that the team clicked better, but that I felt more in control. At that point, it was about me. I needed to get comfortable. Stop questioning myself. The team had perceived my self-doubt. The minute I got in the pocket, everything ran smoother.

I attributed those early losses to decisions I made, second-guessing myself, agonizing over what the rotations should be. I was trying every combination. But I was ignoring my gut.

In the end, I figured it out. Team USA snagged our ninth gold medal against host Japan. Our seventh consecutive win. I became part of a tiny club, along with Pat Summitt and Anne Donovan, of participating on medal-winning Olympic basketball teams as both a player and a head coach.

Griner led the scoring with thirty points. Stewart finished with fourteen. While my rock A'ja knocked in nineteen.

I'd been in their shoes. Taking home Olympic gold in 1996, 2000, and 2004. Yet I got more gratification from that Tokyo win than from my own, because I was a part of fulfilling other people's lifelong dreams. Tokyo was the first medal for Ariel Atkins. For Skylar Diggins. For Chelsea Gray. And, of course, for A'ja.

I could feel the pure joy radiating from them after we clinched the win. When you become a part of other people's history, you carry it in your heart. It sustains you. Bringing those opportunities to other people. The dream merchant of it all.

My whole journey as an Olympic coach reinforced my natural inclination to listen to the voice in my head, to trust myself. To keep using look, sound, feel when assessing myself, along with where my players are and what I need to do to bring out their best.

These days, young people often only want to see the good they've done. They don't want to register anything that needs improvement. In basketball, and in their daily life, they'll veer away from the bad stuff, create blind spots. *I don't want to look over there. I don't want to acknowledge what's happening here.* Our job is to reveal a little peek of it, so they ascertain nothing is as terrible as it seems.

I see myself as a blend of old and new school. I'm less

censored than in my younger years. Yet I explain myself more. I'm conscious of the time we're in. The expectations. Whether it's as a coach, a scout, a front office worker for a WNBA team, or a manager of a business, the value of meeting folks where they are is not only immeasurable but practical.

I used to start the season saying, let's sacrifice being on social media. I wanted my team's full focus. The larger culture is convincing young adults that fame is king, that all you need is a viral social media moment, or a certain Instagram aesthetic, and every door will open for you, and cash will rain from the heavens. In the face of that messaging, it's hard to convince them to go to the gym or run laps, to do the repetitive, grinding work that builds a team and, with it, character. But I soon realized that as much as I wish it weren't the case, social media is an immense facet of their lives. They can't function without their phones. I shifted my POV, softened my stance. We met in the middle.

I approach every player as a person first. You can't plug and play, X and O a human being. I pay attention to every interaction. If something looks, sounds, or feels off, you've got to address it, the sooner the better.

For example, I've seen players internalize a sharp look I flash them at practice, then watch as it dampens their game. Rolling the eyes, pursing the lips, sucking the teeth, avoiding eye contact—those signs tell me something's going on. I'll ask my players, "What's up? Why are you reacting that way? Let's you and I get to the bottom of it." I'll coax the reason out of them, and they'll confess, "Coach, you hurt my feelings." Then I'll explain what I was after, or what I meant, and we'll work it out, face-to-face, human to human.

My cousin Twain, me, and my brother Eric

Third-grade class photo

Fourth-grade
class photo

Sixth-grade class photo

At a hotel pool during an out-of-town tournament with top players from the Philly area

Pitching for the Dobbins Technical High School softball team

Twelfth-grade class photo

Any given Sunday at St. Andrews Fellowship Baptist Church

With Muhammad, my Police Athletic League coach, at City Hall as Mayor for the Day *(City of Philadelphia, Department of Records, City Archives)*

Me in our Raymond Rosen housing projects home

High school
graduation
photo

Nikki McCray and me at Disney while playing for the 1995–96 USA National
Team

University of Virginia graduation

Daedra Charles (far right) and me being welcomed by our French team

Pastor Golden and me at church working in the Vineyard

WNBA media day with the Charlotte Sting *(Garrett Ellwood)*

Grant Hill and me at
the 1996 Olympics

Lisa Leslie and Mom at the mural
ceremony

Me at
Niketown
Chicago

Nike mural located at Eighth and Market Streets

With Mom at the mural dedication ceremony

With my 1995–96 USA National Team teammates and Mom in Philly after an exhibition game

In Philly after the 1996 Olympic gold win

Opening ceremony at the 2004 Olympic Games in Greece *(AFP)*

Media availability after national team practice

Coaching on the sideline at Temple University

(Courtesy of Temple University)

Bill Clinton, me, and Dick Riley (Secretary of Education during the Clinton administration and two-time Governor of South Carolina) at a ceremony announcing the Richard W. Riley Collection at the University of South Carolina
(University of South Carolina)

2004 USA National Team in Greece before we won gold
(Bob Thomas/Popperfoto)

Christmas–Mom's favorite holiday

Champ Staley. My boy's first Christmas, 2017

Uncommon Favor
(Steph Chambers/Getty Images)

I want these young women to feel safe with me. To know they can lay it all out there. I appreciate they're scared I'm going to lose respect for them if I see the real person underneath the facade. To that I say, I'm here to help you take off some of the weight that's on your shoulders, to give you the best chance to excel at two things—academics and basketball. If something's in the way of your being great at those two things, then bring it here. Let me help.

Many coaches opt to ignore player drama, not get involved, and focus exclusively on building their game. Separate church and state, so to speak. To me, that erects roadblocks to trust. I believe allowing an issue to fester only leads to a bigger infection.

At South Carolina, we create momentum by communicating. We explain our whys and whats to our players in real time. Addressing issues when they occur. We don't give them the option to go back and ruminate about what we meant by this or that. We handle situations in situ, get them aired out and move along.

My feeling is if you don't address issues, you're inviting the disconnection to grow, and when you allow it to grow, you find yourself midseason trying to win basketball games while simultaneously trying to dig yourself out of a hole that months before could have taken a five-minute conversation to handle.

Communication isn't easy. Anyone in a relationship knows that. Some people may not want to listen to what you have to say (okay, most people), but if you cater your messaging to the individual in a way that it can be received, they'll hear you. Now, that doesn't mean that they won't smirk, or sigh. They may not love having to listen. But none of that matters if they receive the message and feel heard themselves.

I bring our players into these sticky conversations because I want them to experience what real communication is, and to learn how to have a response. That's what life is about, dealing with people. Sugarcoating and avoidance serve no one. I respect my players enough to tell them the truth.

The door swings both ways. I have what I call an "open mouth policy." I want people to express themselves and not hold back. The caveat is you can't be messy in front of a team. If you have something to say to me, come speak to me one-on-one. Then curse, scream, cry—do whatever you need to do. We can work that out. A young person expressing themselves and saying what's on their minds, that's always a plus, never a minus.

Now, if you break that rule and act out in the group, I will use that as a teaching moment. I haven't had to deal with this in quite a long time, but we have had players who were disrespectful in practice. I used to send them home. Then I thought better of it. I began making them stay in the gym, get on the bike or treadmill so they can remain in our environment and learn.

Letting them leave, that's what they wanted to do. To be on their own terms and left to their own (often literal) devices. I decided it was more productive to make them observe their teammates' more productive behavior. To see, hear, and feel examples of how we are meant to act in a team setting.

Anyone who knows me knows I would sacrifice a game—a small game, a big game, a critical game, no matter the ramifications—to uphold the standards of our program. That's an easy call. That's not a decision that I wrestle with.

You may lose the day, but you'll win in the arena that matters. There is never an excuse to abandon your ethics. I know in my soul what looks, sounds, and feels correct. Sticking with that creates a bigger stake in the whole trajectory of our season and the legacy of our program. In my mind, it's that simple.

Over the years, several WNBA teams have gauged my interest in coming on board. I don't long to coach in the WNBA, never have. If I jump over, I want ownership.

As for other colleges, I seriously considered going to Virginia when Carla Williams became AD. It was hard telling her no. It was my alma mater. Returning to a place so meaningful to my development would have felt incredible. Texas was also on my radar. Texas had everything that I would desire as far as facilities, funding, recruiting. But they didn't come after me. So that was that.

Then there's the NBA. Not long ago, the Portland Trailblazers sought me out. They were serious. They treated me like a real candidate. We scheduled a Zoom.

In advance of the conversation, the idea of coaching in the NBA fully occupied my mind. I visualized being in the locker room, at playoff games. I put myself in those situations and asked: What would I do? How would I react? I'm a Sixers fan, so I envisioned Ben Simmons losing confidence. What would I say to him if he got the yips? What would I advise? Every waking moment, I asked myself, what do I really know about coaching in the NBA?

Then, just as I figured out when I was coaching in Tokyo, I shifted my perspective and landed on what I do know. I know *people*. My coaching centers on forging genuine, solid relationships. I've built a career on understanding human beings, figuring out how to deal with them, all the concerns they're thinking about, navigating their fears, wants, needs, and quirks while not compromising the sanctity of the team.

I decided in the interview that's what I would expound on. How I have instincts that other coaches can't learn. I felt I could make an argument that that approach would benefit the NBA. Look, sound, feel had yet to lead me astray.

In the Zoom, five people were there, firing questions at me. They were heavy on analytics. The league is big into that. Then they asked me about player relationships. How would I handle a superstar?

"I have superstars on my team now. I treat them like people."

I explained that for me, the question is less, how do you rein in the superstars? And more, how do you keep the culture of a team healthy?

I told them I'd forge a relationship with each player and manage them individually. I'd go back to my point guard skills. Spread the love around. I know I'm the coach. They know they're the luminaries. It would become my job to figure out how they take in information, because ultimately you want them to be who they are, while respecting the unity of the team.

During the interview I said, I know these guys don't generally want people in their space. That they don't know whom to trust. My tactic would be to create a family atmosphere. I acknowledged that's hard to envision when you're talking about multimillionaires. But when it comes down to it, they're human.

They want to remember how it feels to be normal. Even the pros want something to believe in, to have an impact.

The coaches who are successful in the NBA, or at any level, humanize their players. They take time to talk to them. They have lunch, dinner. They log the hours. Those same coaches also pay attention to the other, less sparkly team members sitting at the end of the bench. Enable them to see value in themselves.

One questioner got specific. "What about the star player who doesn't show up to training camp?"

I explained that prior to training camp I would have established a relationship. I would have gone out of my way to meet his family, his wife, his grandma, his best friend. I would have met every significant person in his life and built a foundation of mutual respect, so it wouldn't get to that point where he's missing training camp. Relationship building is the key to every win.

The whole time I was speaking with the Trailblazer folks, I jotted down copious notes. I wanted to be certain that if another female coach was ever in the position to apply for a coaching slot with the NBA, they'd have all the details they'd need to prepare.

A couple of days after the Zoom interview, they let me know they had decided to go in a different direction. I thanked them for the experience.

I appreciated the consideration, but in the end, it reminded me why coaching young women remains the ideal scenario for me.

I don't want to massage egos and worry about analytics,

though that's still part of my job. What I want is to change generations through playing the game. What more could I ask? (Well, maybe one other thing. Being inducted into the Hall of Fame as a coach.)

I always say I'm forever indebted to basketball, but what I'm really indebted to is basketball as a vessel. The sport put me in a place and time where I, like the icons I admired before me, could change the culture.

For me, there's just something about women's college basketball that looks, sounds, and feels right.

Respect the Power of Habits

Every year I watch the freshman class try to figure out how we teach basketball. We start with the simplest lesson. We begin from a defensive standpoint. Then, like clockwork, we tick through the routine, build on it block by block. By the time someone's a junior or senior, they know every drill. They've done the same lessons over and over. They're jaded.

I'm there in the mix of it all, glancing between the freshmen who are Bambi on ice, dazed and confused, and the seniors running these exercises like the future pros they'll soon be. The full spectrum of experience. To build a high-functioning team, they all need to land on the same page. And to make that miracle happen, we build habits.

The aim is to groove in certain behaviors so they click like a needle on a record. To eliminate variance. Cultivate the synergy of being arm in arm, sink or swim.

I'm a huge believer in respecting the power of habits. Habits, be they good or bad, are famously hard to break.

Smoking is a habit. Negative self-talk is a habit. Going to the gym is a habit. Practicing free throws is a habit. Biting your fingernails is a habit. Reading is a habit. Eating candy as a snack is a habit. The point being, habits can be your best friend or your worst enemy.

At the top of the season, I have a set of instructions that are easy to follow. Be on time. Communicate. Be respectful. There are other rules within that. For instance, I don't like our players wearing hoodies up in class. We have name, image, and likeness (NIL) protocols where you're not going to miss practice to fulfill a deliverable for one of your deals. You're not going to do anything disruptive on the road.

We stress healthy habits and standards at South Carolina because our players are visible and known. They can't fly under the radar. This can be thorny for them because unlike with other students, if our young women have too much to drink or get in a public argument or skip class or do any other perfectly normal college-student things, there's probably another student watching (maybe even recording) them. There isn't a time when our girls can let their hair down, and that's tough when you're in your late teens and early twenties and away from home and wanting to cut loose at school.

I explain to them, "You're the chosen ones," and that comes with a lot of responsibility. As a coach I need to be as clear as I can about the consequences of not adhering to standards and expectations.

When rocky times happen, I suggest they ask themselves, "What is my why?" Do I want to win a championship? Do I want to learn what it means to be part of a team? Do I want to be in the business of lifting other women up in the future? What are the habits that will lead me there? Hint: it's not scrolling on Insta or guzzling White Claw.

I get straight to the point. If we're disciplined in our habits, we can create our own momentum. Anything else is gambling.

It's complicated with a winning team. We play dynamic, impactful basketball. I've seen these young women seduced by crowd-pleasing. Living for the applause. The crowd goes wild off making baskets, our dramatic offense.

I have to bring them back down to earth and explain that we build our lead on what we're able to do defensively. When you're crushing it, mentally you soften, you think this is how it's going to be every game. Then you backslide.

I get that executing defense doesn't get the fans on their feet like dunking. I know that entrenching habits is tedious. It's natural to get bored. But boredom is an ally. The ability to be bored instead of at sea in an ocean of shiny objects vying for attention is a skill worth honing.

I don't begrudge my players for having their fun. The catch is that a person can only give their concentration to a limited number of outlets. The competition for focus is fierce. If you're goofing around on TikTok, you're not bench-pressing at the gym.

In my calculus, it boils down to revering the game above all else. The game has been too good to me for me to tolerate disrespect. The other day I saw a social media post that said, "Welcome to the Karma Cafe. You are served what you deserve."

I believe it's the same with basketball. If you love up on it, it will love up on you.

These days at South Carolina most of our players are McDonald's All-Americans. Our starting lineup is determined by how they perform as a unit; it's not so much about individual stats. We cycle through nine or ten players who all serve a vital role. Basically, we have players coming off the bench who could start in any other program. The closer we get to naming the starting lineup and designing substitution patterns, we pray there aren't issues. If there are, it's up to me to work them through the disappointment, explain my choices, and make sure my players continue to believe in themselves.

This works if you establish the culture first. It starts with recruiting.

The tendency when interviewing players is to want to show the perfect scenery. I can't fluff it up. I'm completely candid. I describe our program and my style, warts and all. Foretold is forewarned. A lot of recruits want to be promised the world. I explain that's above my pay grade. But I can help you prepare for the next level.

I always ask my would-be players their nonnegotiables, because if we don't have those, let us know so we can move on. I advise them to question themselves, "Can I see myself here?"

I'm inclusive in the process. If a player has three dudes she used to hang with and those are her guys, I'm like, let's bring in your guys. We can all sit down and talk. I want to meet everybody who has your ear. Because ultimately, we're after the same thing. Your success.

I pose the question: Who do you want to text at three o'clock in the morning when you're having one of your worst moments? Which coach do you think will pick up? A school may be a legacy program, it may have every bell and whistle when it comes to facilities, but I remind recruits that you can't hug a building during your dark night of the soul.

I'm just saying, my coaching style is full-service. We're full-service here. But with that attention comes extraordinary standards.

Before you commit, I want you to consider the reality down the line. What if you hit a slump? What if you don't play? What if you don't start? Many coaches do the opposite. They make guarantees.

"You're going to play thirty minutes every game!" You can't tell a kid that. You're going to tell a freshman she's going to play thirty? What about your seniors and juniors? Then what happens when that freshman doesn't start or play thirty minutes? Parents are going to be blowing up your phone. Players are going to tell their teammates, "This is what she promised me." It ruins your locker room. It corrodes trust.

I've never told a potential recruit she's going to start. Not once. I'm not going to shoot myself in the foot with false assurances.

When we lose out on recruiting, I'm cool because I only

want players who long to be here. The experience that they have, not just the winning and the success on the court but the fans who support us—it's like no other place in the country. If you want to pass on that, no hurt feelings. It really is your loss. I say that with zero animosity.

Once a player signs on, we hold monthly Zooms with their family where I remain transparent and up-front. I tell parents that their daughters are experiencing something unfamiliar. They're going from being big fishes in a tiny pond to a sea filled with sharks. It's traumatic to the player and the family because they're used to them being stars.

That's why the communication piece is imperative. Honesty solves problems.

For example, if on game day an individual player is feeling some sort of way about court time, I'll ask them right then how they feel about their minutes. Most of the time the sourness comes because they believe not playing means they've failed in some way. Nine times out of ten, I'm playing the people I'm playing because of what the opposing team is doing. There is no wrongdoing, only strategy.

Sooner or later these young women apprehend the decisions we're making are for the best. When you take the time to be real and open with people, then there's buy-in. There's huge buy-in.

I used to not communicate as much. I didn't invite others into my space. Over the years, I learned that I could be open, and it's okay. I've peeled back layers. I had my own ingrained habits that needed adjusting.

A major turning point came early at South Carolina. I'd

found a new point guard I thought could lead our team. She'd caught my eye playing in another coach's system. I sensed huge potential. Naturally, I went all in, reflexively bombarding her with all the knowledge I'd accumulated as a professional.

The idea was to give her everything that she would need to dominate. Sure, I brought her to tears a few times, but we'd talk through the reasons and motivation behind my approach, and I felt like we were all good.

Then, halfway through the season, she shut down.

The saddest feeling you can have as a coach is when a player powers off. This brilliant point guard had receded, become a shadow of her former self. She quit performing on the court. Her spark extinguished.

I sat with her and apologized for how the season went. I was genuinely sorry. I asked how I could have eased her angst. I reiterated I'd had such high hopes for her game. That I'd regarded her as a linchpin for the team. A way to take our program to the next level.

After I said my piece, my point guard looked at me with sad, tired eyes and said flatly, "Coach, I wasn't ready."

I'll never forget that.

It hadn't once crossed my mind that this young woman wasn't at the place in her life to take on what I was demanding. I didn't pay enough attention. I didn't modify. I was stuck in my old habits, coaching her as if I were coaching myself. That's not what smart coaches do.

One of the hardest things in the world is to look at yourself and be honest about what you see. We tend to excuse our behaviors or justify them in some way. If you employ a strategy that no one understands, it's not them, it's you. Trust me on this one.

When I dropped my defenses and evaluated myself honestly, I found that as a coach my habits tended toward being stubborn, entitled, impatient. I expected the kids to adjust to me. To fall in line and give me what I needed without any regard for what they needed, or who they were.

Since then, I've fostered new habits for myself. Whenever I start a season, I put my point guard cap on and imagine my players as teammates. What would I advise in the locker room? How do I meet them where they are and convert that into success?

I begin by asking them more questions. How do *you* want to play this screen? What do *you* think about this opponent? I may not always agree with what my players say. But they feel like they are a part of the process, they're invested.

I'm fortunate my background managing players on the court translated seamlessly to coaching talent. I isolate the problem. Then work resolves it. As a point guard, I had the literal ball in my hand. I played with luminaries such as Sheryl Swoopes and Lisa Leslie. They both wanted every pass!

I'd tell Lisa, "Sorry I missed you, I got you next time." I'd say the same to Sheryl. That's the job of a point guard. To keep every player motivated and engaged.

This doesn't mean some young people who have WNBA aspirations aren't going to face a bit of distress when they get parked on the bench. As I've lived through it myself, I have empathy. I've been told by coaches that I wasn't ready, or that my ambitions didn't fit into their timeline. I didn't make the

Olympic team my first time out. I didn't start games I wanted to. I've been forced to grow and mature and wait my turn many times throughout my career. When that happened, I had to find other ways to contribute to the team. To not sulk or pout, but instead to do what I had in my power to make this team better.

Armed with that understanding, I know my job is to challenge those young ladies to think more about longevity than game minutes. Celebrate your part now. Make a habit of team.

The top coaches possess a well-developed level of emotional intelligence because ultimately, at the end of the day what you're doing is managing personalities. What we do here is intense. We're in players' lives twenty-four hours a day, seven days a week, nagging them, pulling on them, trying to get them to understand the path forward, to not lose sight of their endgame.

I'm responsible for thirteen individuals and if I allow them to do only as they please, they could harm themselves and they could harm our program. Undisciplined is unpredictable. Favorable habits can quickly be overtaken by unhealthy ones.

To combat that, I condition our players in worst-case scenarios, whether by envisioning them in life, or by a dynamic I create on the court. If they can fight their way out of a nasty situation, everything is simpler to navigate. Triumph creates advantages.

In practice, if we're going over a press breaker, I'll put them in the corner farthest from the basket, double teamed. You get out of the corner, you're going to create a transitional advantage, but getting out of that corner is tough, whether it's via pass fakes, pivoting, or junk passing. There's a lot of skill and thought that goes into figuring out in a hot moment, *How do I get myself out of this situation?*

One of my missions is to unlock greatness in others. My players need to be ready for competition, sure. But I will have failed them if I don't ready them for life. The habits they create with us will stay with them forever.

When you leave our program, move around the country, apply for jobs, intersect with all walks of life, you're going to benefit from having learned how to make a good impression and show up for your team and not just yourself. Say you join the league, everything's totally new to you. The city is new, the coaching staff is new, the terminology may be new. But your habits can be the same old comfortable T-shirt that you've always had.

What I want my players to bear in mind no matter where they land is how the choices they're making today help or hinder where they're going tomorrow.

On that note, I've recently been in multiple strategy meetings with coaches and staff from men's and women's teams fretting over what can be done about NIL. How can we get it under control?

NIL broadly refers to a person's legal right to control their image commercially. Student-athletes used to be prohibited from making deals off their celebrity, but a few years ago the NCAA amended the rules. Ever since, college athletes have been profiting from product placement and sponsorship deals.

For some, the money is significant, a game changer especially for female athletes because women are more prevalent on social media. (LSU gymnast Livvy Dunne nets several million dollars annually from NIL.) If I were playing today, I might have been able to make money off that mean MC Lyte asymmetrical haircut I was working in the nineties.

A lot of ADs and coaches are agitated because NIL income changes the tenor and power structure of collegiate sports. The relationships risk becoming more transactional. They're correct. But the horse has left the barn.

I've raised my hand in those meetings and explained there's really nothing that we can do. The players have all the clout. Instead, we need to think ahead. Have foresight. What are the things that we can do as coaches and administrators to understand what the players want, and deliver that without compromising the program? How can we make NIL a productive habit and a value-add, instead of a distraction or wedge between the players and the program?

NIL complicates the picture because our young women are becoming not only elite players but brands. The rewards are higher, but so are the risks. Growing up and making yourself into a business simultaneously means a lot of strain for a college student. Outside of the football team, our players earn more money than any of the other athletes on our campus. How do you manage all the demands on your time? I don't fault them for feeling stretched and distracted.

For the Gamecocks, NIL went into effect July 2021. As soon as it did, I sent a text out to our team, asking, "Do any of you want me to help you secure an agent? I know a lot of them." I set up Zoom calls with their parents and possible reps. It became a week of twenty-four hours a day getting them secured, because I didn't want NIL to interfere with the season. By October everybody was sorted.

After that, I explained to all the players that without a solid game, the product that is "you" will suffer. I wanted them to maintain the habits we'd grown as a team. I asked them, "What if you don't produce? If you're averaging one-point-two points with no rebounds. Or you're fifty percent from the free throw line?" I pulled out the stat sheets. Told my team members to think ahead. A five-thousand-dollar sponsored post feels like a huge get. But it's nothing compared to a multiyear WNBA contract or a broadcast career.

Sometimes people will sell a virtue or a principle for a short-term win or to avoid being uncomfortable. I'm on the record saying that values and virtues are cheap until you have to pay for them. Then they get really expensive.

I've had a few players over the decades who were resistant to adopting good habits. Like toddlers refusing to eat their vegetables. But I'll tell you what. I'm undefeated. I remind my players of that all the time. I. Am. Undefeated. I will wait you out.

It never fails to make me laugh when these young ladies believe they're pulling one over on us. Y'all running around here, think y'all hiding stuff? We're veterans of this gig. I've been in this for twenty-five years. All y'all's ish is recycled. I know the signs. I know when you're partying, drinking, getting up to trouble. I know when you've fallen in love or are falling out of love. I know when you're depressed, anxious, scared. It's my job to see it, to address it.

I welcome pushback. I'm drawn to the challenges. How do I get this player to understand and see what habits will serve them over time? Bring that trial on. You're not going to beat me at caring about what happens to you.

Now, some of my players won't let their guard down. They're afraid to reveal themselves, because they think I'll judge. They couldn't be more wrong. I think open-mindedness is one of the best characteristics that a coach—hell, a person— can have. In fact, when I recently overheard one of my players say to another teammate, "Coach is the most nonjudgmental person I've ever met," my heart soared.

I've seen it time and again. After we're able to get them out of their own way and they understand why we're demanding certain behaviors and commitments, our players soar like rocket ships. They have their epiphany: *This is what that lady was talking about!* And shit gets easy. They see life isn't as hard as they were making it for themselves.

That's part of being young. Me, older and wiser, I'm advising them how to prune from their lives all the distractions and drama that weigh them down. I had to learn these lessons myself. I know what I'm talking about. You cut the fat, so to speak, and suddenly you discover you have more time, energy, more motivation to devote to the pieces of your existence that are nourishing and future focused.

When nothing else seems to be working, the answer can always be found in reevaluating your habits.

We recently played a terrible game. We got outworked. We won because we had more talent than the other team. But I didn't feel good about it because it wasn't us. So, what did we do? The next day before practice, I made every player tell me why they believed we had that type of performance.

Some of the players said we took that team lightly, which is a no-no. You always respect your competitor. You take the fight to the opposition no matter whom you're playing. You could be up against a squad of marshmallows. You need to approach those marshmallows with respect.

Others said that they felt great at the start of the game, but then they got in foul trouble and couldn't get it together in the second half. A few players admitted they should have played harder. They were honest in their answers.

After listening, I said okay, thank you, now let's get back to our habits. Let's return to doing things the way we do to prepare for a basketball game. We had a great practice, and then, by our next matchup, we were on track.

Make them or break them, habits are fully up to you. Feed the good ones. Starve the toxic ones. Understand you're never too old to grow new ones.

I'm an old dog and I'm still learning new tricks. I'm seeing this now as I coach homegrown phenom MiLaysia Fulwiley. She's a generational talent. Beloved in this community. Everybody in South Carolina has been watching her rule the court since she was in grade school.

MiLaysia's a showwoman. She loves the spotlight during the games, but she eschews that same attention when she's not playing. She's naturally quiet. Reserved. She's intelligent but she doesn't reveal that side of her to just anybody. Her success is forcing her front and center, and she's having to progress more quickly than she expected to. But she's prideful. She doesn't want to need anything. She would rather not ask for help, even if that causes more damage to her.

All I want for MiLaysia is for her to create better habits that will streamline her life. Enable a future where she'll be empowered to do whatever she wants to do. I want her to give more of herself to our team. But she's reticent. And she's young. Nineteen. When you're nineteen, you think you know everything. When you're nineteen you can't imagine being thirty or forty or fifty-five. Or that the choices you make now could affect where you end up at thirty or forty or fifty-five.

I believe in time we'll get there. MiLaysia loves her team-mates. She just bumps up against her inclinations. She didn't say a word when she first came to college. She would not talk. I have to pause here to laugh. The irony that I am coaching a younger, savvier version of myself is not lost on me. I have heard from so many adults who gave their own parents hell, only to see their teenagers return the favor. Now it's my turn in the barrel.

Maybe this late stage in my career is the ideal time to coach a player who echoes so much of the player I was. I feel equipped for the mission. For handling a Dawn 2.0.

When it comes to MiLaysia, I don't rock the boat too much. Most of my interaction with her is one-on-one. I know the way she digests feedback. The other team members probably think I give her preferential treatment, which I don't. They assume that because I don't yell at her. That's not preferential treatment. That's a coach knowing how to reach the player. Very rarely do I call her out in front of everybody. Well, I did once.

MiLaysia didn't like the fact that she didn't play a whole lot in a game and was making a stink about it. I had to let her know that one, it doesn't do me any good to have her sitting on the bench. And two, 90 percent of the time in her short career, she'd been on the floor at the end of the game. You riding the bench means somebody else is getting it done. Be happy for them. Don't say things you will regret.

When I asked for feedback from the whole team about the dynamics after that game, MiLaysia spoke last. She admitted she could have handled things better. That went a long way with the team. A baby step toward a better habit.

As a coach it's important for me to create systems that players can call on in their darkest moments; to instill the resilience they need to fight their way out. If you can't dive into a new habit, stick in your toe. Then try your foot. Then your calf. If you trust the process, stay hungry, do the work, you will conquer your heart's desires. Yes, there will be some suck along the way. It's part of your journey to becoming exceptional.

If I determine a person is a detriment to our team habits, to our principles, to our standards, they must move along. Now, I give everyone multiple opportunities, not just one, not just two, not just three, *multiple* chances to course correct. If they can't or won't, I choose team.

I'm always going to choose our program over any one person. It's unfortunate when you know you're going to hurt a young adult, end their playing dreams. But if they've had opportunities to pivot and haven't, they need to be okay with being cut. Choices have consequences. And that's a lesson of its own.

Many members of my team have shared that their friends ask, "How can you play for her?" I have a reputation for being demanding, tough, uncompromising. Sometimes the words used to describe me are NSFW. My standards are known to be high and my tolerance for slacking and shirking are low. When my players share how intimidating I seem to outsiders, it always makes me smile. Facts are facts. I'm not the coach for everybody. Really, I am not. Like, seriously.

Often, it's the parents resisting my methods the most. (They have their own habits that need breaking.)

When I got into coaching, parents were older than I was. Now I'm older than they are. The style of child-raising has evolved from strict to lenient. Parents are friends with their kids, something my folks would find bizarre. They also helicopter over their children, wrapping them in cotton wool so they never get wounded or fail. I'm not here to say that's a good or bad thing. What I can say is that when their daughters come to me, my attitude is different.

I warn my players, your parents don't want you to be uncomfortable, and they do everything in their power to make sure you don't feel the pain that they felt growing up. I am the direct opposite.

I want you to go through a breakup. I want you to have a crappy game. I want you to bomb a test. To be challenged physically, mentally, spiritually. To find yourself stuck in a bad month or even a bad season, because from those moments, growth takes place.

Mistakes are how you learn not to repeat harmful choices. Evolve into independent women who make wise decisions. Break bad habits.

Baseline, I tell every player, "I love you enough to allow you to hurt."

If you can't fight through or function in that distressing space, that's just not basketball. Being great isn't good enough.

Now, most parents would tell you they don't have favorite children. *Lies.* Your favorite child is going to be the one who does what you ask them to do. I'm teasing, of course. Yet, I can't say that I don't prefer players who listen to me the most. Perhaps not coincidentally, those players are also my most successful.

Columbia local A'ja Wilson was the number one high school player in the country when she graduated. South Carolina was on the come-up, but much bigger programs were chasing her. I felt in my bones that as a top recruit, she could be the player who really pitched our program into the future. Signing A'ja at home would help legitimize USC basketball.

There was a moment when she was deliberating leaving for another school, and her mother said, "Well, then you go down there and tell Dawn freaking Staley that you're not going with her. You deliver that news, because I'm not."

We put A'ja in a position where it was hard for her to tell us no. We'd built a great crowd, we were making it to March Madness, inching closer to the Final Four. Between her mom and me, she was getting pressed like a panini. It worked.

A'ja came on board and with her stellar contributions, we won the NCAA title. Now she's got a statue at the Colonial Life Arena, and her jersey is retired. If she wanted to move home, she could run for mayor.

Aliyah Boston is another player who was rock solid, her character unimpeachable. Aliyah shares that Kobe mentality.

Kobe was a greedy athlete in the best way; he wanted it all. Aliyah wants that, too. To etch her name in the books.

The first interview she had when she came to South Carolina, she was getting compared to A'ja, and she said to me, "I don't want to be A'ja Wilson. I want to be Aliyah Boston."

Actually, Aliyah achieved some goals A'ja didn't. There aren't many players who develop in front of your eyes, rising higher every season. Aliyah somehow dominates while staying sweet. She's a rare combination of lethal skill and Miss Congeniality.

I give all credit to their parents. They ingrained solid habits in their daughters well before they crossed my path. Neither A'ja's nor Aliyah's mother abided any nonsense. They made my job easy.

At the end of the day coaches can only control standards. A coach's responsibility is to be as consistent as possible in their habits while navigating the habits of the unique players on their roster.

Nowadays some young people equate caring with giving them what they want, instead of giving them what they need. Without fail, I am going to give them what they need to be successful. They can hate me in the meantime. I'm cool with that. I don't need that approbation to do my job. Popularity doesn't move me. What moves me is sending my players into the universe ready for anything.

A tight-knit bond doesn't happen with every member of the team. That's okay. It doesn't need to. I remain available. The offer of me in their corner is theirs for the taking.

I've had the benefit of doing this for a long while now.

I've had multiple players leave South Carolina, then come back to tell me how grateful they were for the valuable habits they developed while playing on our team.

When people ask what my best days as a coach are, they assume I'll say when we win a national championship. Three titles in seven years feels incredible. But the days I love most aren't ones on a basketball court at all. They're the graduation ceremonies, followed by the WNBA draft.

Graduation day is bittersweet because it means the birds are leaving the nest. Yet I also see it as a promise fulfilled. For some of these young women, obtaining their college degree is a feat that can not only change their lives, but do the same for generations of their families. I rarely cry during graduation, but you will see me shedding tears during the draft.

Graduating from college is within your control. You've done the work; you've got the grades. There's a formality to it. Hearing your name called at the WNBA draft hits different. That's a lifelong ambition that they put as much work into as they did to earn their diploma. They bled for it, sweat for it, sacrificed so much to make it so.

It's never far from my mind that only a small percentage of women will go to the WNBA. Each draft day, I see my players overcome with emotion as a stranger says their full legal name out loud, and it hits her like an arrow that everything she's forgone was worth the sacrifice. The habits paid off.

I can't help it. The relief and sweet gratification of that moment bring on uncontrollable tears. On draft day I feel full.

Give What You Have Within

I was not born a dog person. My canine personhood snuck up on me in the form of a beagle mix named Ace.

Ace came into my world via my niece Mikayla, who volunteered to dog-sit a nine-week-old puppy during one Christmas break. Weeks, then months went by, and Ace was somehow still with us. Eventually, I figured if the dog was going to be here, I needed to get him his shots. The shots turned into getting him neutered, which turned into daily walks, which turned into Ace insinuating his furry, waggy self into every aspect of my life.

Ace was a kindhearted, spunky animal. He had the longest ears. He also had, I would sadly discover, serious health issues. Ace often struggled to walk. He would seem disoriented, almost like he was drunk. After multiple veterinarian appointments we ended up at the neurologist. They did some testing, and when the results came in, I was told that Ace had a rare brain disease.

In my life, I make it a point to never give up on people. Change is always possible. Miracles happen. You don't know what you don't know. I applied that same hopeful philosophy to Ace.

He was only six months old. The vet told me there remained a slim chance he might outgrow his symptoms. So, I did everything I could after that. Special vitamins. Organic food. Ample fresh air and exercise. Whenever I walked him, I'd wince as he tried, time and again, to clear the low curb. He'd waddle and lunge himself over, doing his best as I cheered him on. "You can do it, Ace! Good boy!" He wanted to live life so bad.

On his rough days, I would send videos to the vet clinic, imploring them, what more we can do? By the end, Ace needed twenty-four-hour care and attention. I'd stay home from work, tending to him. I clung to hope. I kept thinking he would turn the corner. He was still trying, really trying, to live. If Ace wouldn't give up, there was no way I would either.

Many months into his battle, during yet another visit to the vet, the doctor said to me point-blank, "You've done all you can." At this stage, I was holding Ace's tiny body up when he had to pee. Wrapping my hands around his torso so he could walk across the grass. The vet explained he'd wanted to give Ace a chance to heal, for his brain to mature. But it hadn't. And it never would.

The recognition of what was to come hit me like a battering ram to the ribs. I'd never had a dog. I'd never experienced the unconditional love, the easy, happy devotion, the unique bond that forms with a creature who counts on you to be their everything, trusts you in a way no other human ever could. Dogs see us as the people we wish we were. We think we're raising them, but really, they raise us.

The day we put Ace down broke me inside. I sobbed for hours. I kept thinking of him pushing and striving to be a normal dog, the pureness of his desire, the way he never quit. It moved something in my heart.

Months after Ace crossed over, while I was still moping around with grief, Coach Boyer announced, "I'm going to get you a dog of your own."

I instantly pushed back. "I don't want a dog. If I wanted a dog, I would've had a dog by now. Ace wasn't even supposed to be my dog. I. Don't. Want. A. Dog."

Boyer ignored me. She isn't one to back down. She'd seen how much I loved Ace. She sensed, correctly, that caring for a dog was good for me.

Soon enough, puppy photos started blowing up my phone. Cute pictures of this fur ball, that fur ball. Among them were snaps of a litter of Havanese puppies from a woman an hour away from Columbia. Eventually we paid this woman a visit and I cuddled a pair of newborn pups, one cream and another black with white markings. My heart melted. I expressed guarded interest in the cream-colored one.

As the pups grew into adoption age, I'd get pictures and updates. When the litter reached maturity at twelve weeks, I drove back out to visit the dog I expected would become mine.

Boyer had already paid and reserved the cream-coated puppy as a gift. I'd arrived at the house eager to see my new dog when the oddest thing happened.

I walked in, and the white and black puppy rushed over to me. He was wagging and wiggling and acting as if we were already best friends. Then he climbed into my lap and stared deep into my eyes. How could I say no to that?

That was in December 2017. Every day since, I've told Champ, "Thank you for choosing me to be your mommy." We had an instant bond. He chose me. And I chose him. Champ even wrapped himself around my neck on the ride home. Draped his petite fuzzy body across my shoulder like a stole. I knew I was a goner after I let him kiss me on my face. I couldn't stop smiling.

When I registered him with the American Kennel Association, the name Champ was taken. I had to name him Champion, putting dashes in between each letter: C-h-a-m-p-i-o-n Staley. The first day home, he retrieved the ball, brought it directly back to me. I thought, this is cool. I'd never had a dog that I called my own, let alone one who could perform tricks. Then reality hit. I had a dog now. There was no going back.

Choosing to bring Champ into my hectic schedule felt like a massive responsibility. I'll admit I was scared. You can't return a pet. You can't swipe left when the going gets tough. I'm stretched thin. I have onerous demands on my time, a stream of people counting on me at all hours of the day. Nervous, I questioned whether I'd be up to the task of being a dog mom.

My college coach, Debbie Ryan, was visiting when I picked up Champ. Unbeknownst to me, Debbie secretly ordered me

BarkBoxes to help me out, one a month for the first year of Champ's life. Inside were treats and toys and training guidelines explaining what to anticipate from your pet at each stage of development. Housebreaking, chewing, teething, when and what they should eat. It was ideal for a by-the-booker like me. I dove into dog-rearing like I was prepping for a tournament. I made charts and graphs. I researched. I googled. I did every single thing that experts advised I should. Well, almost.

During crate training, I brought the kennel into my room, vowing that Champ would never sleep in my bed. That's what the trainers recommend. Keeping your pup in his own domain.

Being a rule follower, I crate-trained him. When I'd say "night-night," Champ would toddle in there. That didn't mean he liked it.

One day I left Champ in the crate so I could go to the movies, only a couple of hours. He'd be all right, I figured. Halfway into the film, I could not concentrate. I felt guilty, even though I wasn't doing anything wrong. All to say, the crate lasted about two months. (Maybe not even two months.) Champ now sleeps wherever Champ wants.

People tease me that we're codependent. It's true that Champ is with me all the time. He comes to practice. He naps in the USC offices. He hangs out with our other coaches and players. He's so popular, he has a social media presence. Sometimes I get asked about him at press briefings. When we're alone, I talk to him. You can't tell me he doesn't understand.

Ironically, looking after Champ, as much work as it can be, has calmed me down over the past seven years. He's a distraction from the grind. He doesn't care if we lose a game. He doesn't care if the team has a bad practice. He's steadfast. Grateful to be at my side, regardless of my mood.

They say we don't deserve dogs, and that's a fact. Dogs are so much better than we are in all the ways that count. Loyal. Expecting the best. Living in the moment. Excited by the smallest treat. I almost can't remember my life before him.

From day one, Champ's been my calm in the storm, my rock. I never imagined I could have this type of bond with an animal. I have a soft heart, but I keep that to myself. I don't like signs of weakness. Boyer jokes that I lack empathy. I don't think that's true, but I will confess that Champ has allowed me to show compassion in areas that I probably wouldn't have before. With my players. My colleagues. My friends. Dogs crack you open. Without a doubt.

These days, I've grown more receptive to letting the softer side of me show across the board. The folks who knew me back when call me "Charmin" now. I guess I've come to understand the benefit of sharing vulnerability. Not too much. Let's not get crazy. But in some cases, my opening myself up can lead to awareness for others in need.

I've seen this with INNERSOLE, my charity that gives new sneakers to children who are homeless or in need. I've experienced it in my partnership with Aflac, too, when I visit children's hospitals to meet with pediatric patients. During one such visit in May 2023, I spent time with a young lady named Blakeleigh, who was surviving brain cancer.

After an afternoon of activities, we ended up at the arts and crafts table making matching beaded necklaces together. I made mine using pastel multicolored beads, with letters spelling out my name. Blakeleigh got a real kick out of that. I put the necklace on before I left the hospital, and I've worn it every day since. (Not so long ago she gave me a second necklace, just in case the first one breaks.)

Keeping the necklaces on 24/7 wasn't something I planned to do. But I found it meant something to me to wear them. Then, after we won the 2024 championship, I met with some children diagnosed with sickle cell. I sat with another young boy and coordinated my necklace colors with his. I keep that one on, too. The three strands of beads drape across my clavicle like the best kind of statement jewelry.

Sometimes we think our lives are so important and so busy and so filled with the impossible. They aren't. Not compared to the pain and struggle of illness. The anguish of seeing your baby suffer and being unable to heal them.

No matter where I go, people ask about the beads, and that's kind of the aim. The necklaces represent children and families fighting for their lives. For me, they are a material reminder. A constant tether to reality. I put my hand on them, I think of those kids, and every other task in my day shrinks and becomes very, very small.

When folks hear why I have the beads on and where they came from, I hope it offers them perspective, too. I hope they keep those children in their prayers.

We're so often in the dark about the truth and depth of another person's sorrow, unaware of what they're going through. When I reflect on how many people at any given time are privately battling their demons, external and internal, my brother Pete is never far from my mind.

Back home, Pete was the sweetest kid on the block. Like I said, they even called him that in the neighborhood. "Sweet Pete." His given name was Anthony. Pete's disposition was gentle, a born nurturer, a pleaser.

When he was around twenty years old, Pete fell madly in love with a gorgeous girl. They moved into an apartment together. Set about to playing house. Then she began experimenting with drugs. Soon enough, Pete was experimenting, too. Before he knew what was happening, addiction took over his life.

Dealing with Pete's drug dependence, as is the case for the millions of people who go through it, was a dark, frightening place for our family. When Pete was at his worst, it was upsetting to have him around. We all loved him so much. But we couldn't trust him. Pete had become a good liar. He was stealing stuff, selling stuff. We were forced to be on guard. We had to hide anything of value when he came by the house. I had an autographed jersey from Michael Jordan. Some other jerseys from a bunch of Hall of Famers. Petey stole them all. Sold them for drug money.

I recall one time when Pete was at our house with my dad, and we decided to get something to eat. Pete was there sitting on the couch, and my dad said, "Pete, come on, time to go." Pete wanted to rest. He was tired. Lonely. My father shook his head. "I can't leave my house unattended while you are here." My dad ushered Pete to the door. My heart broke watching my brother leave, walking into the cold into God knows where.

My mother had a harder time setting boundaries with Petey. He would come around asking for money, say he needed food. Often, she'd slip him some cash. My mom didn't know how to help him. She didn't know how *not* to help him. She stayed by his side on his worst days. Never cut him off. None of us did. He was a part of us. He was family.

After years of using on and off, my brother got to the point where he was tired of living that way. He was homeless by then. He still worked. Drugs never stopped Pete from working. He made his jobs fun, "even though they weren't," he used to say. Eventually, Pete joined Narcotics Anonymous. He threw himself into the program, got a sponsor, and got clean. When my dad passed away on December 1, 2006, Pete relapsed. But he pulled himself out again quickly. He finally had the tools.

When my brother passed away in 2021 from a stroke, he had just celebrated twelve years of sobriety. He had come around. At the end of his life, he was happy.

Like I said, I make it a point to never give up on people. Everybody has something worth fighting for inside of them. One should never abandon those souls life has taken by storm. Instead, reach out a hand. Help steady them.

No matter where my journey leads, I don't want to divorce myself from the swim of humanity. I don't want to be immune to the grief of others. I want instead to give what I have within.

I felt called to do so when my sister, Tracey, first began feeling ill in the spring of 2020. It was the early Covid times. No one could differentiate between a normal flu and what we later learned was the coronavirus. Medical facilities were overwhelmed. Although Tracey was unwell most of April, she's tough like me, so she carried on, telling herself it was nothing so terrible she couldn't manage.

A month later, she was alarmingly weak. Her cough incessant. She located a doctor to see her amid the Covid chaos, but he told her the tests she needed would take a long time to greenlight through insurance, and she'd be better off going to the ER and receiving them ASAP. Tracey drove herself to the emergency room, where they conducted the tests. After a few hours, one of the doctors walked into the holding area and announced to my sister that the results were in. They'd revealed she had cancer. Leukemia.

It was that sudden. Tracey was admitted that afternoon.

Stunned by the news, I did what I always do in crisis. I activated. I started calling people. I called Sylvia Hatchell, because she'd had leukemia, too. I called Duke coach Mike Krzyzewski, aka Coach K. I called my doctor. I called the Cleveland Clinic oncology department. I called Robin Roberts. I reached out to every person I believed could help in any conceivable way. All I wanted was to arm myself with information and locate the best care I could find for Tracey.

I kept a notebook throughout the process. Phone numbers. Advice. Tips. Doctors. Conversations. Every detail scribbled inside. I was trying to control a situation that felt uncontrollable.

When it came to treatment, most of the doctors spoke the same language. They told me the protocol, the variables, the facts on the ground. I won't lie, when I was talking to the doctors, I name-dropped. I used every tool in my kit to make sure they knew that I had a wide reach and I would be watching them like a hawk. That there would be no shortchanging. We ended up selecting a doctor at Duke University. Treatment began at once.

My sister was in the hospital for thirty days. We couldn't visit her inside due to Covid restrictions, but she had a window that faced the front of the hospital. I would take Champ and stand outside and wave at her. Tracey could see me, and she'd wave back, smiling like nothing was wrong.

Tracey was receiving chemo during that month. After that, if she was to survive, she'd need a bone marrow transplant. All our family members got tested. Within two weeks, the compatibility ratios came back. My brother Eric was a two out of ten match. I was a half match. And then, thank God, my oldest brother, Lawrence, was a ten out of ten. A perfect match.

Once you know that you have a match, they start prepping you for the transplant, which requires the doctors to strip your immune system like bark from a tree. This meant my sister had to stay in the hospital for another month.

I would visit Tracey every weekend. Now I could go inside. When I saw her, Tracey would be dressed in street clothes. Never a hospital gown. She was defiant.

"I'm not going to be in here like some sick person," she'd say. "I'm going to get better and I'm going to go home and until then I am going to do what I would normally do and that means wearing proper clothes."

Her mentality was so strong. Tracey was never, not once, afraid. She decided from day one, if this is what we must do, this is what we must do. She took cancer head-on. Her positivity was an inspiration to everyone around her, especially me.

If Tracey was staying upbeat, pulling on her big-girl panties, then I could, too. Her force of will prevented me from going dark. I'd rib her, "Something is going to get you, Trace, but you're not going to die from this." And she'd laugh and nod her head.

When it was time for the bone marrow transplant, I road-tripped with my brother to Raleigh. He had to give blood every few days. He's a funny dude. He was like, "Man, am I going to have enough juice left to survive?" He got dizzy after the first day and needed a wheelchair to haul his butt out to the car. Tracey is the one with leukemia, and he's falling out in the parking lot.

For months various friends and family members and I lived together in a suite at the local Marriott. They gave us a nice discount. The staff couldn't have been kinder. Then, at last, the day came for the official transplant, and we all decamped to the hospital.

In the surgery suite, the scrubbed-up doctors emerged carrying this dinky little plastic bag. It was so underwhelming. The precious lifeblood that was going to save my sister looked like a Ziploc filled with fruit punch.

I was there when they hooked Tracey up to the machine.

"Thank you, Jesus," she said. "Thank you."

That's when she cried for the first time. She let herself exhale that day.

The transplant was a success. What followed were four more rounds of chemo. First round, Tracey was all right. Second round, rough, but okay. That third round, I was visiting for the weekend, and she was a wreck. It was the worst I'd seen her look throughout the entire diagnosis. She had oozing lesions on her lips, inside her mouth. Open sores and a body ache that made it excruciating to breathe. She couldn't eat. It burned to close her eyes. My sister, strong as nails for months, was cracking. We were so close to the finish line. Nevertheless, it was her decision to make.

She elected not to continue chemotherapy.

Her medical team pushed back, but Tracey was firm. A week later, she checked out of the hospital. We had to remain in Raleigh so she could get examined daily. One week, we got a surprise day off. I looked at my sister and said, "Do you want to go home?" We weren't supposed to leave, but sometimes you just need to sleep in your own bed.

We sped away from Raleigh like bats out of hell. Drove home the three hours to Columbia, where Tracey could hug her kids, wash her clothes, be amongst her belongings. Where she could remember who she was before all this started.

The following morning, we rose early and sped back. The medical team none the wiser.

Over the next three weeks, each time we had a break, no matter how short, I took Tracey home. This was during the Gamecocks season. I was missing September, but our amazing staff was taking care of business while I was taking care of Tracey. There are no shortcuts in treating leukemia.

We got uncommon favor. Today, Tracey is in remission. Her oncologist says she was an absolute machine. My sister used to make him laugh. The way she continued to crack jokes, stay upbeat, walk around that hospital like she was touring the mall astounded him. No matter how brutal the treatment, Tracey refused to feel sorry for herself. Nor does she now. We all know that if she'd needed to go on a national bone marrow match registry, she wouldn't be here today. Like I said, we got lucky.

Since my sister's recovery, I've found myself reflecting on how brief our time is on Earth. No one can predict what's coming in the next act. No one knows when they will need to rise and meet the moment. I've never been one to take good fortune for granted, but I'm even more mindful these days.

I let things go that I might not have in the past. I get over myself. I'm gentler with my friends. I take long, contemplative walks in the mornings. I look at the Congaree River, the reflection of the sycamore trees mirrored in the water. I hug the people close to me when I leave town. I place my hands on my beaded necklaces. I snuggle with Champ. I say thank you, thank you, thank you.

Maybe I am Charmin now. Soft as warm butter.

I think about the outpouring of emotion I showed after the 2024 NCAA championship game, something I'd rarely displayed in public prior. I generally keep my feelings on lock. But that year was different. What was going through my heart and mind at that time was too big to contain.

When you're competing for a national championship, or any big goal, you prepare, you plan, you pray, and then you're not supposed to worry. You let Jesus take the wheel. Y'all, I did a lot of worrying. On and off the court. When the season commenced, I was asked to offer three words to describe the team, and I said, "Expect the unexpected." I must have been psychic.

That team did not launch auspiciously. Our success was hardly a given. To start, they didn't begin in tip-top physical shape. Psychologically, a lot of the players were noncommunicative. I would text them, and they'd ignore me. I guess the kids call it "putting you on ice."

They would be late to class or appointments or practice. Gestures of ambivalence, at best, that I wasn't there for. I persisted, meeting them where they were, sharing that our expectations were high, our standards even higher. Along with my colleagues, I taught them the discipline, the habits they needed to meet the mark. Luckily, we got there in time.

When the buzzer sounded and we met the moment in the end, it felt as if my cup had runneth over. There was little I could do other than release all that emotion.

There's a nakedness that comes with exposing your underbelly. You open yourself up to judgment, criticism, ridicule. The public can be cruel and petty. I remember the social media reaction to my crying. Folks were shocked. Some even clutched their pearls.

I've always been a fighter. Philly tough. But on that day, my mother came into my mind. I remembered her infinite wisdom, the advice she gave me when I was still young. *Put down your armor, drop your defenses, embrace the platform that comes with having a spotlight.* My mother always hoped I would give what I had within. Let my innermost spirit shine through.

I feel pride knowing that the times when it's counted, I've done just that.

You're in the Room for a Reason, Now Move It

In 2004, all of the captains of the USA teams gathered in a conference room as part of the standard deliberation over who would be the flag bearer for the Olympic Games in Athens. I was a captain, so I was in attendance. Just before the process, my teammates told me, "You're our choice." Which meant that since I was also a captain, I had to nominate myself. Awkward.

The next step was to discuss and debate every nominee. I listened as other captains ran through their potential flag bearers résumés. Athletes who had overcome life-threatening circumstances. Or rehabbed from devastating injuries. Athletes who beat cancer. People were tearing up as they told their stories.

Then it was my turn.

I had to stand up in front of everybody and make my case for an honor I wasn't convinced I wanted or deserved. It was expected that I list my credentials and achievements, which I did, shyly. I said I had a foundation that serviced middle school girls back in North Philly. I was coaching at Temple University. I was here for my third Olympic Games, where I was, to date, undefeated. Then I sort of shrugged. That was the extent of it.

Once all the twenty or so nominators had spoken, it was time to vote for a top five. When the tally was complete, I had miraculously made the list. When that happened, you could have knocked me over with a feather.

I was gobsmacked. Like, *really?* I didn't even vote for myself. I didn't think I rated compared to the other candidates.

From the top five we winnowed to a top three. This was all happening quickly. Again, I made the cut. At this point I'm looking around the room, like, am I being pranked? When the last and final vote was tabulated, I was deemed the winner. It was official, I would be the flag bearer for Team USA.

I didn't feel worthy of the selection, but the process ended up being a valuable lesson for me about how spotting leadership in yourself is as important as seeing it in others. I needed to learn that I was in the room for a reason.

At the time, the privilege felt so immense it was almost abstract. As I left that meeting I ran into Team USA administrator Carol Callan outside. I told her I'd been voted in to carry the flag for the opening ceremonies. I was reeling. Carol said, "You've got to call home and tell your mom!" I wasn't supposed to share the news, but Carol insisted. "Just keep it quiet," she advised. I rang my mother and revealed the secret.

Mom was proud, but she didn't know much about being the flag bearer. I explained that when they'd introduce the United States at the Games, I would be the first athlete everyone sees. I was in a position of representing not just Team USA basketball, but also every American who was competing.

As an athlete and coach, you aspire to be an Olympian. If you're in the game long enough, you reach for other goals. To win more medals or compete in a second Olympic Games. But I'll admit, carrying the flag representing my home country had never entered my mind as a possibility.

Honestly, the magnitude of it was hard to process. I had been a part of two prior Olympic Games. We as the basketball team always enter last in the opening ceremony. I didn't know what the duties of flag bearer were about, because I'd always been bringing up the rear of the pack. Well, I was about to find out.

When the day arrived, the US delegation gathered in a holding area. Our Team USA uniform was a short navy skirt, a matching navy button-up cardigan we left open, with a red USA shirt underneath. We had a fun cap to top it off. I don't wear a lot of skirts, but I was the flag bearer, so it was what it was.

As we waited in the wings, a serious gentleman approached me and suited me up in the harness and flag. He solemnly explained I was to walk six feet in front of the delegation. I was given a list of dos and don'ts. He said you can't dip the flag as you walk into the stadium. You must smile no matter the reception you receive. Americans are often booed or heckled when competing in other countries.

I nodded. I can do that, hold the flag high, keep a smile on my face. He ended by saying, "We are the USA. Keep your head up and walk tall."

Then, just like that, it was go time. I was anxious as I took my first steps into the stadium, a wall of noise and light greeting me as we merged with the parade of nations. I pushed my shoulders back and stared straight ahead, gripping the flagpole like it was a life preserver.

My team filed in behind me, and I could hear the crowd roar as the men's Dream Team entered Marousi stadium. LeBron James, Allen Iverson, Carmelo Anthony, Dwyane Wade, Tim Duncan. I felt like I was in my own basketball version of a royal wedding. A tidal wave of emotion rolled over me as I listened to the cheers for them, and for all the Team USA Olympians. I had never been so proud to be an American.

While I walked a lap of the arena, I thought about how far I'd come from North Philly. I thought about my high school, our undefeated three-year run, and how that experience lit the fuse of my desire for winning. I thought about my college coach, Debbie Ryan, who was in the stadium somewhere, probably grinning ear to ear. I thought about all my previous teammates and coaches and the lineage of basketball—my mind ticking through all the steps and seasons and strokes of luck that had landed me in this moment.

For me to find myself where I had, the stars had to align. Talent, coaching, no career-ending injuries, no devastating personal tragedy. If any one of those variables fell out of alignment, I wouldn't be here.

As I rounded the curve, I heard chants of "U-S-A, U-S-A!" and could sense the celebration building behind me. I looked over my left shoulder and saw the faces of my teammates lit with passion. Some were crying happy tears. Others were beaming and fist-pumping the air.

I realized I was no longer nervous or anxious. My mother wasn't able to make the trip to Greece, but I felt her presence. I knew back home she'd have a house full of people and a giant spread of food she'd have been up all night cooking. I imagined her glued to the television this very moment, watching her baby daughter lead the pack, flag in hand.

At the end of the last leg, an usher signaled for me to enter the main field with other countries. I took one final glance around. Soaking in the astonishing truth that the best athletes in the world were following a girl from the Philadelphia projects.

It bears repeating: I am my mother's child. She never let us get too high with the highs or low with the lows. She always maintained a certain level of equilibrium. I've tried to do the same.

As you age, you see the way people treat you. You see the way people treat others. You see the way they treat Black people. You see how they treat women. You see how they treat men. You see the whole gamut. My observations have shown me a single person really can change how organizations think and operate.

That day, when I was bearing the flag for Team USA, was one of the first of many times when I've inadvertently brushed up against my power. I came to see that I was put in that space, that arena for a reason. I was there to move the room.

Everybody has the ability to lead. You just have to want to. That doesn't mean you need to be the CEO of a Fortune 500 company, or a pioneering lawyer, or a rabble-rousing politician. You don't have to be Beyoncé. You can be an odd kid from Philly who mastered a sport and was chosen to carry the flag by a jury of her peers.

I wasn't born with instinctual leadership qualities. My journey was one of the silent introvert to the loud messenger. More than once as I've come up in the ranks, I've had imposter syndrome, thought to myself, *Perhaps I'm a fraud.* The more I researched, I discovered, to my relief, that in the main, leaders aren't born but are instead forged. Leading is a muscle you can build.

I know for sure what ushered me into leading was my competitiveness. If competitive genes exist, I have all of them. I want to win at everything. No matter how small the stakes or trivial the activity. Always have. It's the Philly mentality. We're the ones who persevere. Winning isn't simply, "I scored more points than you." Winning is being able to be in a space where the deck is stacked against you, and you find a way. That doesn't mean the results are going to be picture-perfect. But there will be results.

Competitiveness is also why I became a point guard. I wanted to manage the team. Increase the odds of victory. I needed to have my hands, literally, on the ball.

As I matured, and my career went on, I noticed that there were times when I got opportunities, like being the flag bearer, because somebody saw something in me that I did not see in myself. This was never more accurate than with coaching.

From where I sit now, it seems nuts to say coaching wasn't on my radar. But it wasn't until it was. Not before veterans more seasoned and cleverer than I was sized me up and saw a chance to put someone with hidden potential in the room.

These days I believe that I'm a better coach than I was a player. And I was an excellent player. Looking ahead, I have high hopes, but I'm also a realist. I take nothing for granted. If you're in the game long enough, you grow familiar with the cycle of Black coaches who get a shot at running their own programs. If they're successful, they'll continue. If they're not, they're forever relegated to assistant positions. Black coaches don't get a chance to fail twice.

This pattern is partly due to the fact that the folks who are decision-makers often aren't Black. Managers, board members, ADs (CEOS, VPs, commissioners, etc.) run in certain circles, and in those circles, they get advice about whom they should hire. Those circles tend to lack diversity. People hire whom they know. Whom they're comfortable around.

At some point, we need to disrupt that pattern because we are in a space where there are a lot of Black athletes in college and in the pros. Why not promote a Black assistant coach? Give them some latitude and stick with them for a few seasons? They shouldn't be pigeonholed when they're qualified to take the next step.

I'm still usually the sole Black coach at the NCAA Final Four. When there are only white coaches in the marquee games, it sends a message that those are the only folks capable of coaching at the highest level. The Final Four is a recruitment tool. Would-be collegiate players are watching. Donors are watching. If you see two Black women there, it broadens the scope of what is deemed excellence.

We need to bring these dated conventions to the forefront, pose the "uncomfortable questions." You don't get answers if you never talk about it. Twenty, even ten years ago I wasn't being asked about race and opportunity, because there weren't enough of us to field the conversation. Our numbers are ticking up, but we still have a ways to go.

The environment at the SEC is a great example. Four of the women coaching are Black: me, Joni Taylor at Texas A&M, Yolett McPhee-McCuin at Ole Miss, and Johnnie Harris at Auburn. Four out of sixteen coaches is not a great percentage, but it's something we're actively working to improve. We know with the visibility and reach of the SEC, we're able to have a voice and tell a story no other conference does.

You can watch our games and clock with your own eyes that we coaches have the goods. And when young people see us out there, excelling, we're navigating them through a place in history that, if we weren't there, no one would ever know.

In women's college basketball roughly half of the players are Black, and yet few Black women are heading programs. There are a couple more Black athletic directors in the power five conferences, but there aren't enough people who are being intentional about hiring Black women.

This isn't about supplanting other coaches who have long been the norm. We're simply arguing we should be added to the story. Making the case that Black women can flourish on the biggest stage of college basketball. We expand the narrative.

And, with any luck, the vocabulary.

As a rule, you rarely hear Black coaches, male or female, in any sport, referred to as "geniuses." The adjectives describing us aren't about intellect or ingenuity. Often the go-to is that we're "relatable." Because the players (usually Black) "relate" to us. Which, sure, okay. Seeing your world experience reflected in a coach is a good and valuable thing. But no one wins any athletic championship based solely on relatability. It's coaching. We win because we're excellent at all the skills coaching demands.

Then there are the times when I hear references to our team as being overly physical. That vocabulary smacks to me of a certain bias. Most of the time I ignore those comments, starve the flame. But now and again I'm compelled to address them because the chatter impacts our players.

After our 77–73 loss to Iowa in April 2023, I sat at a press conference. I was asked for a status report about our team.

"The truth about our team, good question," I began, taking care to look into the eyes of the assembled crowd.

For weeks, certain reporters had been overheard talking publicly about our program. Some coaches, too. They were describing us in a way that they should not have been. Especially not national sportswriters covering women's basketball. I couldn't let that stand.

I began, slowly, exposing the truth as calmly as I could.

"We're not bar fighters," I said. "We're not thugs. We're not monkeys. We're not street fighters."

I paused, let those words hang in the air, then continued.

"This team exemplifies how you need to approach basketball on the court and off the court."

I kept talking, calling out the hurt caused by those words, the insidious harm when a reporter who holds those opinions is the person writing about our team. I needed to let them know, everyone in that room, that they should cut that nonsense out. Let's not call each other names. Let's talk intelligently about the game.

"You can not like our team," I said. "And you can not like me." But using that language only confirmed what we already knew.

I ended my response with a heartfelt ask.

"So, watch what you say when you're in public and you're talking about my team in particular. Just watch what you say about our team. Because it's wrong. You got young lives who are really, if you really knew them, *if you really knew them*, like if you really want to know other players who represent this game, you would think differently. So, don't judge us by the color of our skin, okay? Judge us by how we approach the game."

I took a breath. "Because I'm not changing," I concluded. "But I hear you. I hear you. I. Hear. You."

As I spoke that last line, I punched every word. I wanted to be clear. I was not going to sit back and let my players be diminished in that way. I was not going to allow those comments to go unanswered. I was going to use the power I had in that space to move the room.

I'm good with having uncomfortable conversations. Frankly, we don't have enough of them. Let's have a conversation about why you feel the way you feel about me or my team. I'd prefer that to the microaggressions (and macro), the coded (and not so coded) language that's used when covering us.

I did that in 2020, after the decision-makers of women's basketball decided that they were going to push Oregon's

Sabrina Ionescu the whole season. Don't get me wrong, she's probably one of the greatest college players ever to play the game and well deserving of the spotlight.

At the beginning of the year, she came in after the Ducks went to the Final Four the previous year. At the same time, the Gamecocks lost one game in November and then never another. We kept this incredible momentum heading toward a national championship run, but it was swept under the rug in favor of coverage for certain players.

Again, not a knock on them. But you must understand, no matter how well we did, the narrative fed to the media never shifted.

I initially kept quiet because I didn't want to be a distraction to our team during the season. Yet, I kept reading, I kept listening, I took notes. The story stayed on Sabrina, and not the Gamecocks being the number one team for nine weeks. To the end, we never received publicity or had our achievement amplified.

Once the season ended, I had a few choice words for these decision-makers. I told them how I felt it looked, not just for South Carolina but for the rest of NCAA basketball, because there were powerful stories on many teams that weren't being shared, other dazzling players who deserved their flowers.

We are a predominantly Black team, with a Black coach who sits at the top of women's basketball. The decision-makers are not used to that. Some fans actively wish it weren't the case. For my part, I can take the prejudice, the stereotyping. It doesn't hurt me. I'm over fifty years old. I'm from North Philly. There's nothing anybody can do that's going to hurt me.

But when you wound my players, that's a different story.

They're just kids. They haven't built up enough resilience to withstand the way they're being portrayed. I see their pain every day. It kills me that I don't have the answers that they want to hear. But I'm not going to let the continued battle against racial and economic inequity consume me, because if it's consuming me, I'm less of what I need to be for them.

So, what I tell them is the truth.

For now, this is the way it is. We're going to have to navigate through this social climate and you're going to need to figure it out, because it's not changing anytime soon. No matter where you are. The law of averages, the way this world is made up, it doesn't favor us.

I tell them to know their value. But don't expect others to grant it to you. And be ready when they try to tell or sell you something different.

As for those peanut gallery critics, I'd ask: How are women supposed to play basketball in a way that makes you feel comfortable? How are we meant to win without upsetting your expectations?

In January 2018, the Gamecocks played at Mizzou. The whole game was twitchy. The energy palpably off.

Mizzou players and fans were amped up, hostile. A'ja Wilson fouled out after nineteen minutes. I was ultimately ejected for arguing with what I saw as dubious calls and failing to substitute a player quickly enough. We lost by nine points. When we exited the court, my players were heckled by white fans.

"You're thugs, just like your coach."

Back home, we were left to simmer in that unsettling experience until our rematch at the end of the month. During that game, all the buried damage and antipathy erupted in an on-court fight. Two Mizzou players were removed from the game. We managed to calm the scene and come back to win. Only to learn shortly after that Mizzou's athletic director, Jim Sterk, made a postgame appearance on a local radio station where he said the not-so-quiet parts out loud.

The host said to him, "I was really thankful you got out of Columbia, South Carolina, alive on Sunday night."

Sterk replied, "It wasn't a great atmosphere. It was really kind of unhealthy, if you will." He continued, adding, "We had players spit on and called the N-word and things like that. It was not a good environment, and unfortunately, I think Coach Staley promoted that kind of atmosphere, and it's unfortunate she felt she had to do that."

I was livid. I couldn't process that an AD at a university could say that at all, let alone about me. Calling my character into play. You can love me or hate me, but my integrity is not something that is up for debate. Nor is the character of our program or our fans. Painting Columbia as some kind of war zone you're lucky to escape alive? Ridiculous. *Their* players were called the N-word? By our team, who was all Black? The whole premise of his commentary was absurd on its face.

After I recovered from the shock of what had been said, I mobilized. There had to be something I could do to correct the record. We sent Sterk and the school a letter asking him to apologize, but he was not forthcoming with any apology. They provided no response to the letter at all.

In SEC circles, there was pressure to sweep the whole ugly

incident under the rug. Just move on. But I could not let him get away with spewing falsehoods and defaming me and my program. Sterk wasn't backing down. I knew I wouldn't either.

When I spoke to the press the next day, I told them, "The accusations are serious and false, and they will be handled in a manner reflective of those facts."

Then I sued him.

I may have been silent as a girl. But I was a grown woman now, with a platform and a microphone. And I was going to be heard.

Trust me, we didn't want to make anything litigious. We tried to remedy the situation outside of the legal realm, but after being ignored, we were left with no other option. The defamation suit, filed in February, was about principle. I'd built my reputation over decades. I wasn't going to permit one man to sink it or impugn our school and our fans with falsehoods. I was tired of turning the other cheek. Of high-roading. Like my mother, I chose to fight for what was right, and in this case, that was correcting the record and shining a klieg light on what Black women endure day in, day out, regardless of stature.

Sterk and the University of Missouri quickly settled for fifty thousand dollars. Half went to my nonprofit, half to pay the lawyers. He was fined another twenty-five thousand by the SEC for violating the conference's code of ethics.

In his public statement he said, "I made comments in a local radio interview that were construed to suggest that Coach Staley promoted the negative experiences of racial epithets and spitting. I do not believe Coach Staley would promote such conduct, and I sincerely apologize to her for those comments."

I wish I could say the whole episode didn't affect me. But that would be false. It cut me deeply. Confronting the tide of inequity can be exhausting. Seeing the pain in my players' eyes. Knowing that tomorrow, around some corner, more of the same awaits.

What I knew to be true then, as sure as it is now, was that these times are not for the weak. Your strength must spring from your character. I followed my heart because I knew the truth. I did what my mother would have wanted me to do.

As I say to every player, you have to know who you are. The sooner you can get to who you are, what you stand for, what you believe in, the sooner your path is revealed.

My hope is that more young women choose the path of coaching. I want them to grow our game because it's breaking through to a wider audience, and we need to keep people wanting more. I want them to embrace and project their power. The impact you can have as a coach, as a vehicle for change, far dwarfs any personal accomplishment. Yes, it feels amazing to be the best in your field. But nowhere close to how transcendent it feels to lift others to be their best.

There is longevity in giving back. By that I mean, the impact of your efforts stretches far into the future. The tail of influence is long. It isn't tied to a single season or award or medal. It's an infinite forward throw of goodwill and hope.

You never know how far the groundwork you lay will travel. Which little girl in the stands is going to watch your players and imagine for the first time a different life for herself.

Which father is going to root for your team while his son watches.

Which former player will never forget who she is because she was part of a team of collective greatness.

Which woman is going to listen to you at a press conference and realize that she, too, has value and a voice to fight for it.

I was a withdrawn kid. People would tell me to speak up, but I wasn't quite ready. Now look at me. I can speak in front of hundreds of people, and although that's not my most comfortable moment, I know that when I share my story or speak my truth, what I'm saying resonates with people.

Women's ball has a rich history. Decades of players paved the way and put up remarkable stats. We as a culture tend to rally around a certain type of representation to the exclusion of others. Or worse, in contrast to others.

Honestly, the media struggles with how to market Black people. To them I say, just stick with the facts. If you just stick with the facts, it's easy to market a team. To my players I say, as long as we keep making history, they're going to have to say something about us.

When you see injustice or you observe things that aren't right, you feel it in your stomach. It knocks the wind out of you. My impulse is to react. I'm going to say something. I'm going to do something. I will never be afraid to speak out about what I see as inequity or prejudice. I'm not going to subject myself to living in a box. If I have a belief, a perspective, I'm going to share it. Whether that pulls people in or pushes people away, that's not really on me.

I'm a Black woman first. I coach young Black people. I constantly ask myself: Am I doing right by our players? Are they learning? Are they understanding? Are they being equipped to navigate the world as Black women in our society?

There are conversations that we must be able to have, exchanges that enable all of us to grow socially and culturally and to foster empathy for each other's point of view. I mean, that's the way the world's supposed to operate. That's how we build unity and collective power.

Perspective matters. It enriches whatever situation, whatever company, whatever team you happen to be on. When I'm able to give my perspective, it's different from what's traditionally in the room. That's a good thing. If you have only one perspective, you risk being blindsided or clueless. You may not always agree with those perspectives, but if you're listening and aware, everyone at the table can feel a part of the picture. Giving somebody else the mic enriches the whole chorus.

Representation also matters. I know it's a cliché nowadays, but the truth remains. Whether it's girls having the WNBA to aspire to, or young female political science majors having Vice President Kamala Harris as a role model, representation ensures they have something real to reach for. Only with representation will disparities in health, education, and economics narrow. I pray over time it's enough to open the door to a new and kinder world. To ensure that in the future Black Americans can walk, drive, or jog freely without fear of being profiled, harassed, or killed.

I remember watching the murder of George Floyd. Seeing him lifeless on the street under the pressure of another man's knee shook me to my core. Viewing that footage, I was acutely aware of how easily that could have been my father, or one of my brothers, uncles, fellow coaches, or friends.

The brutality and clarity of the facts of George Floyd's death stirred the country to protest. To me, his murder was both shocking and not. Our country has a founding history of racism and violence, one yet to be fully reckoned with. With George Floyd, we watched someone die at the hands of a police officer who could have easily gotten up. Who could have allowed George Floyd to breathe, to live. Instead, that officer chose to kill a man in the street. Before the eyes of the community. Before the eyes of God. The impunity of that privilege is staggering, but vital to grapple with.

As I wrote in an essay at the time, "What do you say to young people who've seen that video? What do I say to my nieces and nephews? What do I say to my players? They're like my kids. I want to give them at least some hope that what happened to George Floyd will never happen to them, but I don't have the words. Because the truth is: That very well could happen to any of us."

My status as a national championship coach, the fact that I have won gold medals for this country, received numerous honors for my community work, traveled the world and reached a certain level of celebrity, has not protected me from being racially profiled or treated unkindly because of the color of my skin. Whenever this happens, I am jolted, taken aback. But I shouldn't be.

There is no level high enough, no accolade prestigious enough, no bank account big enough, no medal shiny enough to eradicate deep-seated bias. There is also no margin for error.

Women of color, immigrants, LGBTQ+ folks—no one in those groups ever gets to falter or fail. I am reminded of Michelle Obama's speech at the 2024 Democratic National Convention.

"Most of us will never be afforded the grace of failing forward. We will never benefit from the affirmative action of generational wealth. If we bankrupt the business or choke in a crisis, we don't get a second, third, or fourth chance. If things don't go our way, we don't have the luxury of whining or cheating others to get further ahead. No. We don't get to change the rules, so we always win. If we see a mountain in front of us, we don't expect there to be an escalator waiting to take us to the top. No. We put our heads down. We get to work."

The work, we all know, is without end. The question for all of us is how do you continue to get up?

Recently, I was in an airport, and I was standing to board when the airline representative ignored me to speak to the person behind me. When I said, "Excuse me, I'd like to board," she eyed me up and down. "Are you first class?"

I nodded, calmly saying, "That's why I'm in the line."

The gate agent pursed her lips and scanned my ticket. I wanted to say more, but instead I took a deep breath and told myself, *I'm not going to let this ruin my day.*

Bias is learned. It's taught and is conquered only through love. When I'm my best self, I think about how painful it must be to harbor hatred for someone you don't even know. To wander around in a cloud of fear of the "other." Hatred always says more about the hater than the hated.

When I'm not my best self, I'm weary. I'm angry. I'm impatient.

Most of my players are Black. Their parents are Black. What happened in Minneapolis to George Floyd, what takes place all over this country, it's a part of the fabric of our lives. I personally can't simply shut down and coach or "shut up and dribble," because we're impacted. We're human beings. We have feelings. It hits home for our players. And for me.

I want to be a person who stands on the ground of doing what's right and saying what's right, even when the masses believe otherwise. I will continue to do that because if you're a leader—I'm not talking only a Black leader, I'm talking any leader—you must take stands.

I mean something to these kids. For me to sit on my hands during the time in which our country was rife with unrest? That's not me and it will never be me. I'm going to continue to speak out on issues that count, so I can be a voice for those unable to raise theirs.

I always tell people I don't have a political agenda; I have a human agenda. We must find the humanity, the love for one another. You can agree to disagree about issues and continue to respect a person for what they're bringing to the table.

I see the big picture because, well, I have to. Black women can't expect greatness to be enough. We look ahead. We go long. We pitch ourselves into the future, one hand behind us, pulling other women up.

When I tell the media every season that my purpose in coaching is being a dream merchant for young people, it's not exclusively about basketball. A dream merchant helps a person navigate the sea of life. I want this world to be different for the young people I coach. I've constructed my existence to be a beacon of hope for someone who looks like me, who grew up like me, to help them see that whatever they dream, they deserve.

But I can't change the tide. I can't chase the darkness away. I can't defy gravity.

What I can do is be real. Honest. I can fight. I can kneel for justice when everyone else is standing.

And when I'm in the room, I can move it.

God Bats Last

My grandma cooked meat on Sundays. One Sunday afternoon, when my mom was a young girl, my grandma directed her to run to the butcher shop to pick up the makings for supper.

When my mother arrived at the store, she waited patiently in line, then, when it was her turn, politely requested the meat she needed. The butcher, a white man, returned from the back with what my mother noticed was spoiled meat.

My mother, all of fourteen years old, shook her head. *No.* She asked for a fresh cut. She explained she couldn't take that meat home, that her mother would be none too pleased, that she'd be in trouble. The butcher ignored her, slid the rotten meat across the counter, his hand outstretched for payment.

My mother stood her ground. Even as a teenager, she was not one to back down. Though it might have been better in that moment if she had.

My mother and the butcher stared at each other, neither moving an inch. After a beat, my mom turned and left, the spoiled meat sitting there, unbought. She hurried back home, the butcher shouting behind her to never come back.

When my mom arrived at home without the meat, my grandmother wanted to know why. As my mother painted a picture of the scene at the butcher shop, my grandma grew tense. This was rural South Carolina in the fifties. Not far from where I live now. My grandma knew what it meant for a Black child to publicly defy a white man. She knew the danger, the threat now looming over her family like a rancid fog. She knew, also, exactly what in that moment needed to be done.

As soon as she could, she packed her daughter's bags and sent her on a bus to Philadelphia to live temporarily with her sister, Sarah, whom we called Big Mama.

I was young myself when my mom first told me that story. It wasn't framed as a lesson. Just an account of how she came to live in North Philly. We didn't have to have the "sit down at the table" talk about racism in my house when I was growing up. We all knew what it was.

Time is a funny thing, isn't it? That I find myself thriving in the very state that drove my mother into exile is an irony I never forget. That she was able to return to her home, her place of belonging, when I came to work at South Carolina was a full-circle moment made possible by social progress, the civil rights movement, myriad changes seismic and small, but also, in large part, by faith.

No matter what life threw at my mother, she never lost faith.

Back in Philly, every time the church door opened, Estelle Staley was there. I mean, it seemed as if revival week was every week. My mom would go to services every day she could. She was the Walmart greeter of the church. Welcoming all comers into the house of the Lord.

As fate would have it, none of those comers ever seemed to be anyone in my family besides me. Sure, sometimes my sister would attend, and every so often, my brother Eric. But as the baby of the family, I was forced to go. I was the youngest, and a girl, and my mother wanted me near her. (That worked out fine for me because I could guilt her into buying me candy as a snack between services.)

Church was my mother's happy place. She was never more joyful than when she was at St. Andrews Fellowship Baptist Church on Ridge Avenue (before it moved to Wayne Avenue). We had around three hundred parishioners. Every one of them knew my mom by name.

Most kids view going to church as a punishment. But I didn't. Not entirely. I had to wear skirts. I had to wear stockings. That was not my favorite. But the pluses outweighed the negatives. My mom and I were close, and I adored getting time alone with her, without my siblings around. It felt special. Now, I didn't want to get up early Sunday morning, but once I was there, the welcoming energy filled me up.

I was particularly into the revivals. Bishop Seymour would

come for a week, and I loved to hear him preach. I appreciate reverends who take you to a time and a place, then wrap it around and bring it back, almost like the loop of a song. Bishop Seymour made people connect with scripture. It's hard to put a sermon together. You must hold the attention of kids and adults, bring them all along for the ride in their respective imaginations. Then send them home with the desire to be better people.

At church I had a totally different set of friends from the ones I had in the neighborhood. I sang in the choir. I didn't sing solos or anything like that. I despised being front and center. I preferred being in the background. I told the choir director I could sing the loudest there, hidden from public attention.

We were called the Golden Specials. The pastor's name was Johnny Golden. My mother was in the Golden Voices, the senior choir. She was also a trustee, an usher. She cooked meals for after service. She did everything. She loved her church family like they were blood.

My mom's best friend was the first lady of the church. When she passed away, Mom grew close with her daughter, Joyce, who remains in our lives today. Joyce is an evangelist, too. An incredible preacher. She can move you. She can make you laugh. We talk every week. I like to keep people in my life who give me perspective. She's known me my whole life. To have the continuity of that relationship is rare and valuable. When Joyce gives me advice or counsel, I listen. Sometimes she visits me in South Carolina, and we talk about the old days.

Before games, Joyce texts inspirational messages. Like: "May you continue to trust you. Welcome back on the court." Or "No looking back, except to say, look at what God has done.

Let's get this win in Jesus's name." Or "I know this is a big game, but our God is bigger. What he's doing through this program is and will forever be a testimony to him." Those kinds of passages calm me down.

They also remind me of my mom. They're the kinds of things she would say. It's comforting that although my mother isn't here, her spiritual guidance is. Sometimes Joyce will text, "Staley is looking down on you proud." "Staley" is what she called my mother. The thought of her watching over me with pride is a balm like no other.

As a child, you don't really understand the power of God. You sit in the pew, fidgeting, half listening. I sat with my friends. If we were too loud, Mom would give me the eye. You knew what that meant. The sermons kind of washed over me. I recall our pastor repeating certain phrases every Sunday. One prayer that he used to say was, "Thank God for waking me up in my right mind." I never knew what that was about until I got older. Then when my mother went through Alzheimer's, that prayer really landed.

It's profound that a phrase I heard as a girl in church would end up becoming a prayer that fortified me through my biggest challenge as an adult. I think frequently about how if my mom had picked a different sibling to take to church, my point of view would be totally different.

As much as I was called to basketball, I think my mother was called to preach. Unlike me, she never answered her calling. Even Bishop Seymour would tell her she had "the gift." My mom, she "worked in the vineyard." Meaning, she logged her hours at the church.

She volunteered, helped the needy. We were there for the three services that took up all of Sunday. Knowing her, I think she did all this activity to avoid preaching. She wanted to be certain God knew: maybe I'm not heeding this calling to be a pastor, but I'm going to do all this other service right here, so make sure I make it in the pearly gates.

I joke, but the point is, my mom was very, *very* faithful. Unfailingly loyal to the church. You couldn't say one bad word about her church family, her pastor, none of that.

I was fine coming to services, but in no way did I want to officially join the church. When you join, you've got to walk up to the front, stand there in front of everybody while they pray over you, ask you deep questions. *Do you accept the Lord Jesus Christ as your Savior?* You can't simply nod your head. You've got to project your voice. I was twelve. At that age, I was trying to project invisibility.

After you survive all that, now you've got to do stuff in the church. I would have to work in the vineyard. There was Bible study and service. Choir rehearsal on Saturday. Saturday! Saturday was for basketball!

Now, my father never went to church. When he and my mom met, they both partied a bit. They were young and in love. As time wore on and kids entered the picture, my mother and father grew apart. One major reason was he never stopped partying. It was almost like he chose one side. And my mom chose the other.

After she opted to go the religious route, my dad resented her decision. He despised that part of my mom's life because he wasn't in it, though that was his own doing. When

I was a kid, it seemed to me that the more my father loathed and trash-talked the church, the closer my mother grew to God.

Faith buoyed her. My mother needed somewhere to place her energy. She knew what she was going to stand for and what she was not going to stand for. Her religion became a challenge for her to live right, to do right, to pour her grace on other people. I watched my mom expand who she was through church, where everybody seemed to feel her spirit, her presence. Kids would gravitate toward her. Anywhere my mom went, she never met a stranger.

My folks stayed together until I graduated from college. They never got divorced, but they separated shortly after I completed my degree in May. My mom left our family home by summer. It was a deal she made with herself. To wait until all her kids were adults. Once my mom moved out, I moved out, too. I rented an apartment, and she rented one of her own. And that was it for the Raymond Rosen projects and the Staley family. But it was not the end of her faith.

My mother wanted a better life, and she found it through her church family. Although her daily existence was in a project in North Philly, her spiritual life was far broader and richer. As a child, when you read a fairy tale, you're transported to the place you're reading about. I think for my mom, her church took her places. It bolstered her strength. She had a scripture for every twist and turn of life. It was the code that deciphered her reality.

Faith made her life make sense.

These days I'm in church a lot less. I listen to sermons online. I read the Bible on my phone. My favorite scripture is Psalm 23.

The LORD is my shepherd; I shall not want. He makes me lie down in green pastures. He leads me beside still waters. He restores my soul. He leads me in paths of righteousness for his name's sake. Even though I walk through the valley of the shadow of death, I will fear no evil for you are with me, your rod and your staff they comfort me. You prepare a table before me in the presence of my enemies; you anoint my head with oil; my cup overflows. Surely goodness and mercy shall follow me all the days of my life and I shall dwell in the house of the LORD forever.

I mean, it's so perfect. When I recite it, I feel mighty because it's such a powerful scripture. Why do you think I'm able to deal with anything thrown my way? He leads me down the path of righteousness. He restores my soul. The outcome is always: You're going to win. Even though you lose, you still win. Even though I walk through the valley of the shadow of death, I fear no evil. Thy rod and staff, they comfort me.

I'm a woman of abiding faith. I don't judge people who aren't. It's not for me to judge. Folks can live their lives any way they want. For me, though, God has always lit the path.

The amount of success that I've had, it's not the norm. I'm the only individual to win the Naismith Award as both a player and a coach. I'm the first Black coach to win three Division I national championships. Ten gold medals as an athlete, including three Olympic and two FIBA world championship gold medals, one bronze medal, and seven international invitational titles. Where I come from, that is not supposed to happen. That's not in the script.

I suppose there are plenty of rags-to-riches stories of athletes who have been the chosen ones in their families. The exceptions who broke the mold. You can think it's all you. But I never have.

It's part of why I offer game-day devotionals. I have from the beginning of my coaching career at South Carolina. When I started posting them on social media some years back, it caused a bit of friction. I received letters from this organization, that organization. Places that want to keep church and state separate. I represent the university, they argue, and posting a printed-out devotional on a bulletin board is forcing my religion and my preference on my players.

What they don't know is that each season I ask every player whether a devotional offends them. We have all religions represented on our team. Atheists, too. If a single player ever said they were bothered by the posts, I wouldn't do it. I'm not here to offend anybody. That is not my makeup. That's not my character.

I also post inspirational memos along the lines of "What we do is who we are!" and "Do not focus on the emotions of points, rebounds, and championships won. Focus on the people you are and how you will leave this place better than you found it. That is what legacy is."

At the end of the day, if what I'm posting isn't for you, then keep scrolling. Tune me out. If it is for you, I hope you get something out of it.

I found myself in similar hot water after my postgame interview with ESPN's Holly Rowe, when we defeated the Iowa Hawkeyes in 2024.

She started by acknowledging that you don't see tears from me often, and asked, "Why tonight?"

Weeping, I told her, "We serve an unbelievable God, we serve an unbelievable God. Uncommon favor, unbelievable. So proud, I'm so proud."

We'd just become the tenth team in NCAA Division I history to finish the season undefeated. I was overcome with emotion and gratitude. I told her I was super proud of where I work, super proud of our "fams." I credited Winston Gandy with doing a hell of a job on our scouts. I gushed about the players, how they locked in and executed and believed they "weren't going to be denied."

"I'm so incredibly happy for our players," I continued, speaking my truth to Holly. "They etched their names in the history books when this is the unlikeliest group to do it, and sometimes, I mean God is funny like that, he's funny. He rips your heart out and he makes you believe the unimaginable. Thank you, Jesus!"

Almost immediately some corners of the media picked up on my comments and took issue with my overt Christianity. One Daily Beast article quoted Annie Laurie Gaylor, copresident of the Freedom from Religion Foundation, arguing that I "have no boundaries when it comes to pushing religion on a captive audience of students dying to please [me]." Other hot takes accused me of undermining my players in some way by offering glory to God.

Anyone who knows me sees the silliness of that argument. To praise one entity is not to subtract from another. It's not a pie being divided into pieces. Never mind that I credited coaches, South Carolina, the parents, the fans, and the team in the very speech they were decrying.

The bottom line is that being a coach at South Carolina is just a part of who I am. It's not my total existence. And to those who tear down the faith I hold dear, I would say it's easy to be an arsonist. It's much harder to be an architect.

My leaning on my Christian values is not new. I've always walked the walk. I defend my players when I feel they are being unjustly criticized. I speak out on issues that other coaches avoid, such as gender equality and racial bias. Earlier that same championship weekend, I fielded a question about trans athlete participation, one of the most politically fraught (and weaponized) topics in women's sports, and unambiguously and unapologetically stated my belief: If you identify as a woman, you should be able to play.

It's my faith that makes me strong enough to enter the fray every day and advocate for a better, fairer, kinder world. When we are blessed with winning a national title after an undefeated season, trust me, I am going to give all the thanks.

In my work, I meet a lot of people who are adrift. So much of what we live through is out of our control. The world can be dark, so, so dark. If I hadn't grown up in the church, I probably would've lost myself. The way my life has evolved. Traveling all the time. The pressure to deliver. A nonstop schedule. The pace of modern life can swallow you up.

For me, faith provides the guidance I need to keep moving

forward. It helps me be a better mentor. It fortifies me so I can be a wiser navigator for young people and for anyone else who's watching. I may be a leader, but faith will always be the thing that leads me.

As I found when Covid hit.

The year 2020 was gearing up to potentially be the biggest year of my professional career. The team we had was a coach's dream. A combination of veteran leadership and rookie energy stacked with all-Americans who gelled with each other, shared the ball, had unbelievable chemistry and an undeniable will to win. Coaches don't get this type of team very often. It was a unicorn roster.

I was shopping in Asheville, North Carolina, when I saw the headline on Twitter. *The NCAA to cancel the women's and men's 2020 basketball tournaments.* I stood motionless for a few seconds, attempting to take in the gravity of what those words meant. I scrolled my feed, hoping it was a hoax, only to find it confirmed. I let loose a few expletives and took a seat on a nearby bench to gather myself. To grieve.

Disappointment washed over me for our fams, our student body, the city of Columbia, my staff, our program, and, of course, our players. We were so close to another national championship. I had the parade route mapped in my mind. It hurt to imagine all those shared dreams and years of work washed away in an instant.

A few days later, or maybe weeks—it's all a blur—I received the news that the 2020 Olympic Games in Tokyo would be postponed. I would still get my chance to coach the Olympic team eventually. But it was a second blow. I wasn't sure how to escape the sorrow that enveloped me.

Months went by. The shock and pain subsided. Replaced by the encompassing emergency of the pandemic. I found myself more thoughtful about what was happening in the wider world, and as I did, my disappointment turned to thankfulness.

During that (forced) hiatus of uninterrupted time, something significant dawned on me. I needed to slow down. To sleep. To not burn the candle at both ends. To disconnect from my devices and all the daily responsibilities I carry.

I rediscovered my humanity in the overwhelming vulnerability we all faced. I reacquainted myself with the things that count.

Since then, I've made it a priority to reconnect with loved ones. I talk to people. Not texts or emails. Real face-to-face conversations with meaning. I ask questions and listen to the answers. I examine who I am. Where I stand. I lean on my strengths and strengthen my weaknesses. I trust in God's plan.

Life doesn't come with instructions. What it does come with, however, is a series of trials and errors that afford you the opportunity to learn, build, and grow. And sometimes, in the best times, it brings you full circle, back to the heart of the matter.

When I moved to South Carolina, I brought my mother with me. She was initially reluctant to leave Philly. After I officially accepted the coaching position, I took her house hunting. We drove around Columbia, and she'd point out her old haunts, such as the corner beauty parlor or the hardware store. We shopped for furniture. We visited with her sister. She went back to her childhood church.

Years later, her great-grandchildren would visit, and they'd tell me that Grandma was forgetting things. She wouldn't remember she was cooking. She'd leave raw chicken in the oven, neglecting to turn on the broiler. My mother was very tidy. She washed her clothes daily. But dirty clothes had begun to pile up in corners and on couches. All signs something was amiss.

I decided to move in with her for a while to observe her behavior up close. She'd take a bath and grapple with exiting the tub. Towels festered on floors. Sinks went unscrubbed. My mother, who'd never met a challenge she couldn't face, who was fearless, dignified, stalwart, a force of nature, was now seemingly unable to complete everyday tasks.

I immediately took her to a neurologist, who suspected Alzheimer's. He ran her through a series of tests. He gave my mom three words she had to recall. He drew a circle on a piece of paper and asked her to add the numbers of a clock.

My mother tried, but her numbers didn't go all the way around. They were squashed in a semicircle.

The doctor posed a series of questions. "What's today? What year is this?"

"I don't know," my mom would answer. She'd throw me a side eye, mutter under her breath, "Dawn, tell me the answer." Or she'd wave and say, "Bye-bye." She still had her sense of humor.

Then the neurologist asked her who was the president of the United States.

"Barack Obama!" my mother exclaimed. That one she knew.

I told President Obama that story when I went to a dinner

in New York where he was the featured speaker. He didn't know me at the time. The WNBA invited me to represent the franchise. At the end of the event, I beelined up to the president; I probably wasn't supposed to do that, but I was like, screw it, I won't get this chance again. I introduced myself and told him about my incredible mother, who was suffering from Alzheimer's, and how the only answer she could remember on her diagnosis test was that he was the president. I told him I appreciated him for that, for his impact on my mother's life. He smiled and thanked me, and I moved along.

After that initial appointment, the neurologist advised that my mother could not continue to live on her own. I moved her into my house, hired a caretaker from ten in the morning to ten at night every day. I installed security cameras so I could make sure my mom remained safe. On the live feed, I'd watch her pack up her whole room. Empty the closet, stack her clothes, make the bed. Unsurprisingly, my mother hated being dependent.

Sometimes she'd come downstairs and announce to me, "I'm ready to go home." I'd have to calm her, walk her back upstairs.

Now and again, she'd leave anyway. Open the door and sneak out when the caretaker wasn't looking. If I wasn't home, I'd have to sprint back from the office or call my neighbors to intercept her. I ended up installing double locks on the doors.

As the months wore on, my mom became scared, paranoid. She would call at sundown, convinced someone was peering in her window. "They are out there, Dawn," she'd whisper. "They are."

After a year, she'd declined to the point where it wasn't healthy or safe for her to be in a house at all. She never wanted to go into a facility, but the time had come. That was a terrible day. Mercifully, it wasn't long before my mother didn't know where she was. Her mind wasn't capable of landing on a place or time. But she recognized me. She knew I was her daughter till the end.

Watching the woman I loved and respected most in the world deteriorate into a shell of her former self was the ultimate test of my faith. *Why her? Why now?*

I had to remind myself that she was the one who led me to God in the first place. She had prepared me for that day via the life that she lived and the example she modeled. The potency of her belief system set the stage for me to be okay with her passing. More than okay. To see the other side of it. To know she went to a better place, and that she's all right now.

Earth has no sorrow that heaven cannot heal.

My mother passed on August 10, 2017. She was seventy-four years old. Her funeral services were held at the Bethlehem Baptist Church in Woodford, the town where she was born. She was survived by her children, nine grandchildren, two great-grandchildren, and eleven siblings. Every week since, I have lilies, her favorite flower, delivered to my home.

I have a painting of my mother hanging in my main hallway. In it, her hair is white and cropped, curls framing her face. Her forehead is scrunched, cheeks round, eyes twinkling above a wry smile, as if to say, *I see you.* She looks happy and wise and at peace.

I find myself quoting her often. All the lessons she instilled, even ones I didn't like (maybe especially those), I hear coming from my own mouth. My mother lives on in many ways, but most tellingly through my voice.

She taught all of us kids to be kind, patient, and charitable. To understand differences and, rather than fear them, to embrace them. She made sure we knew that God is the only judge, and he works alone.

I remember her saying to me that anyone can choose to move the world forward for better or for worse. If we do nothing, not only can we not complain, but we are complicit.

Now that I'm older, I better understand the ordeals that my mother endured to keep her family together, trials that would have tipped the average person into desperate survival mode. Estelle Staley knew how to live in the moment. She would not be crushed by history or circumstance. She held her head up high and continued to live life on her terms. She was never defeated. She chose joy.

Because she was able to do that, we as a family were, too. Her fortitude became our foundation. We believed in ourselves because we saw our mother hold on to her power when the whole culture said she should have none.

After winning my first national championship in 2017, I cut down the net. It's a tradition. A few days later, I went to my mom's house and draped that same basketball net around her neck. She smiled, even though she thought it was a bit silly.

Looking at her in that moment, I was reminded again that I

am not the blueprint. I am a living, breathing example of all who came before me, and in their honor, and in honor of my faith and the grace shown to me, I will continue to serve.

I'm going to salute God. I'm going to remember when I'm at my worst, he's at his best. And I'm going to try, every chance I get, to praise the uncommon favor he has shown.

Be Kind to Yourself

In October 2016, I ended up in the emergency room.

My chest was tight, I couldn't fully inhale. A stabbing pain pierced beneath my left breast. I underwent a battery of tests to pinpoint the crisis, praying I wasn't experiencing a heart attack.

An MRI revealed severe inflammation in my heart's pericardial sac. I was diagnosed with acute pericarditis, a swelling of the heart lining. It's a condition, often exacerbated by stress, where you can't do anything but breathe. And even breathing feels like a knife plunging into your chest. The medical protocol is to keep your heart rate low. If your heart beats faster, it bumps against the inflamed lining of your heart, and the pain intensifies.

The day of my diagnosis, the doctor said, "This is not going to go away on its own. You're going to need to stop coaching."

Stop coaching? I nearly laughed out loud.

I explained I used to be an athlete. Athletes deal with physical setbacks all the time. We find a way to cope. As an athlete, you fight through. We trust the body can heal itself. If it doesn't, that's a problem for another day.

The doctor said pericarditis is different.

"You don't understand this condition. It's debilitating. It takes a long time to heal. You can't simply will yourself to get better."

He recommended that I be hospitalized, stop flying, quit exercising, maybe undergo surgery.

"Okay, I'll think it over," I said, knowing there was zero chance in hell I would do any of those things.

We had an incredible team. We were just getting rolling. I wasn't going to not see the season through.

I ignored his advice. Tried to ignore the pericarditis. I managed the disease with medication and regular checkups. No surprise, it got worse.

I'd double over at practice. Shout orders at the team from the sideline. Confront referees from the bench. It ached to stand up, to pace. I couldn't carry my own bags through airports.

I'm not one to show weakness. I made the choice to keep my condition a secret. I didn't want anything to disrupt the sanctity or mood of the team. I plowed through. I never missed a game. I coached through the hurt.

In 2017 we won the championship. No one was the wiser.

In the end, I only divulged my diagnosis when my face grew distorted from the steroids I was taking. I needed to tell people. They deserved an explanation.

I used the six-month break between seasons to heal. But my doctor had been correct. Treatment was a long haul. It would be three years, up to right before the pandemic, before I got my clean bill of health.

In my calculus, gutting out my diagnosis was something I had to do that I didn't want to do to get our team what we wanted. I've navigated through injuries. I've navigated through losing seasons. I've navigated through all of it. I'm a survivor.

In retrospect, though, it would have been wiser to share what was happening in my life with more folks, ask for more support. There is such a thing as being too headstrong.

As with everything, I blame North Philly.

Had I grown up anywhere else, in any other way, I'd be half the person I am. To me, when I say I'm from Philly, it means there isn't anything that I can't accomplish.

I remember getting puzzles for Christmas. Puzzles are a cheap present. Some holidays, it was all that my family could afford. It was fine with me because I loved puzzles. I was good at them.

I'd sit there for hours, eyeballing the pieces to discern where they fit. I had a sharp memory for where missing pieces belonged. I enjoyed the hunt, thrilling at the discovery of a hard-to-find match and the satisfaction of laying it in.

Most of all, I loved seeing the final result, everything snapped neat and tight, all that mental effort resulting in a perfect, harmonious, knit-together picture.

Little did I know then that the way my brain worked, moving tiny pieces of colorful cardboard around, would take me to places and realms as fantastic as any of the images I saw once those puzzles were complete.

At this point in my life, I'm often asked what advice I'd give my younger self.

Well, for one, I would tell myself to have gotten the right-size sneakers so my toes wouldn't be all knobby. I've got large feet for my height. I wear a ten or ten and a half. I think I was supposed to be taller. I've got big feet, big shoulders, big hands, a big head. When I was younger, I didn't want my sneakers to look huge, so I would get the smaller size, take the insole out, ram my toes in. All of that was an error in judgment.

I'd tell younger Dawn to treat people with kindness. To be patient. Mostly with herself.

I'd say be brave. Lead with courage. Ward off fear with everything you have inside. Fear will immobilize you, keep you stagnant.

I'd say success will not come easy, but it will come. And when it does, you will challenge assumptions. You will find your audacity. You will change history just by existing. You will move the room.

I'd remind myself that setbacks and defeat are gifts. Stand in the face of discomfort and smile your brightest smile. What's delayed is not denied.

Finally, I'd say, at the end of it all, make your belief in yourself greater than anyone's disbelief.

My legacy is as an odds beater. If my example is to do one thing, I want it to encourage people to live without the fear of judgment. I want people to feel free. To find their passion. Because once you do, life opens up.

If you're not able to dial in on what resonates with your soul, you get bored, you're unfulfilled, sometimes angry. It really is a shame. Because life is hard enough. The everyday ins and outs of existing drain you. They beat you down.

The way you fill yourself back up is with purpose. Not money. Not social media likes. Not the envy of your friends and neighbors. Not promotions. Not shopping. Not drugs or alcohol. The path to fulfillment is through work that lights you up. You want a life that means something.

In my entire career, I've never experienced a time when I thought, *I don't want to do this anymore, it's too much*. The minute I do, I'm going to exit stage left. I'm not going to wrestle with it. Or debate. Or phone a friend. Once coaching stops making sense, I'm out.

"But what will you do?" pals ask. "Whatever I want to do," I answer.

Maybe I'll pick up golf. Tinker around in my garage. My needs are simple.

The only thing I pray for at the end of my career is the choice to be my soul's desire. I want to leave the way I came in. Eyes open, heart full, ready.

When I started in the game, I did it because of how it made me feel. I loved competing. I loved playing basketball. It gave me hope, it gave me a way of surviving, a way of life. It was so wholesome in my mind.

Because of that, people were drawn to me, then later to what I achieved. You can sense when a person is doing something from a pure place. I had no ulterior motive. I played, and now I coach, from a base of unadulterated love.

Basketball swallowed me up, embraced me, and I'm forever indebted to it. I don't take any of my good fortune for granted. I hope I've done right by my blessings. I pray that I've inspired faith in those who need it, because I believe that's what I was meant to do.

On the (very) rare days when I fantasize about an alternative career, I imagine myself as a singer. Like Adele. Or Whitney Houston. I'm mesmerized by vocalists of their caliber. I'm drawn to how they command the room, tell a story we can all hear, making us feel alive, like we belong to something.

That's what basketball did for me.

From my very first moment on the court, basketball made me feel like I belonged. It told me everything I ever needed to know about myself.

It forgave me my sins. It gave me a voice. It kept me free.

ACKNOWLEDGMENTS

First and foremost, I want to thank God for the gifts, guidance, and grace that have shaped my journey. Without faith and perseverance, this book would not have been possible.

To my family—your love and support have been my foundation. Mom, your strength and resilience inspired me, and your unwavering belief in me has carried me through every challenge. To my siblings, my biggest fans and fiercest protectors, thank you for always keeping me grounded.

To Rene, Lisa, Angela, Renee, and Beverly, you are my extended family, my support system, and my safe space. Thank you for the laughter and the late-night conversations, and for always keeping me humble and true to myself. No matter where this journey has taken me, your love and friendship have been a constant source of strength.

Acknowledgments

To my teammates, you are my sisters in sport and in life. Every game, every practice, every challenge we faced together shaped the leader and competitor I am today. To my coaches, mentors, and those who pushed me beyond my limits, thank you for seeing potential in me even when I didn't see it in myself. To my Temple University family, Temple is where I grew, where I learned, and where I built a foundation that shaped my coaching career. To my assistant coaches, players, and everyone who supported me, thank you for being part of my journey. The lessons I learned at Temple will always be a part of who I am.

To the University of South Carolina, the fans, and the entire Gamecock family, your love and dedication have made every step of this journey worthwhile. Coaching this team has been one of the greatest honors of my life, and I am forever grateful for the opportunity to lead, learn, and grow with such an incredible group of young women.

To my fellow women in sports, players, coaches, and trailblazers, you are the reason I continue to push forward. This book is for every young girl who has ever been told she couldn't, and for every woman who refused to accept that answer.

Thank you to the team at Simon & Schuster and the Atria Publishing Group, especially Charlamagne Tha God and Nicholas Ciani, for their belief, patience, and dedication since 2022. Thank you to my literary agent, Simon Green from Pom Lit and the Excel Sports Management team for making this happen. Thank you to Allison Glock for helping me bring these lessons to the page.

Acknowledgments

Finally, to my readers, thank you for taking this journey with me. Your support, encouragement, and passion for the game fuel my purpose. I hope this book inspires you to chase your dreams, break barriers, and never back down from a challenge.

D awn Staley is head coach of the 2017, 2022, and 2024 NCAA Women's Basketball champion South Carolina Game-cocks, a three-time Olympic gold medalist, and a Naismith Memorial Basketball Hall of Fame inductee.